SHE'LL BE RIGHT (NOT!)

A Cybersecurity Guide for Kiwi Business Owners

DANIEL WATSON

CONTENTS

INTRODUCTION

YOU'RE LIVING IN A DIGITAL WORLD. We all are. From the tools you use to promote your business to the tools you use to operate your business, I can bet that you rely on technology every step of the way. The thought of not being able to log into your company systems or access your emails is scary – so most business owners just try not to think about it!

Tapping into technology helps us work more efficiently, communicate, and grow – and you and I both benefit from it.

But what happens when that technology is turned against you?

In just one quarter of 2019 alone, the reported financial loss from cybersecurity breaches across New Zealand was a massive $6.5 million, while total losses by both individuals and businesses throughout 2018 were $14 million. From spam emails to ransomware, viruses to accidental data loss, cybersecurity issues are everywhere – and they're costing us all.

* * *

Ransomware
A type of malware (malicious software) that encrypts a victim's

files so they can't access them, often used to demand a ransom from the user.
How much would you pay, and how much data can your business afford to lose?

* * *

CYBERSECURITY: A GLOBAL CHALLENGE

You know how interconnected the world is now. Just think how easy it is to buy something from Amazon in the States, stream the latest movie releases, or message your friends on the other side of the world. Technology is an incredible resource connecting all points of the globe.

So it's pretty unsurprising that cyberattacks are also a global phenomenon.

When I think of global cybersecurity, I can't help but think of global shipping giant Maersk. In 2017 they were hit by a massive cyberattack with a cyberweapon called 'NotPetya'.

* * *

Cyberattack
A deliberate attempt to breach the IT systems of an organisation or individual, usually to benefit from disrupting the victim's network.

* * *

As many of the computers in their Copenhagen office and across the world were affected simultaneously by a ransomware attack by Russian hackers, Maersk staff quickly realised that every computer could soon be infected by this malicious software. The malware, installed via a single computer and able to get through due to old operating systems, not-very-effective software patching, and insufficient network segmentation, was designed to be completely destructive. It spread across the entire network, irreversibly encrypting data and the very records that told a machine how to operate.

"I remember that morning – laptops were sporadically restarting and it didn't appear to be a cyberattack at the time but very quickly the true impact became apparent," said Lewis Woodcock, head of cybersecurity compliance at Moller-Maersk.

It took the company two hours to shut down the entire global network, and employees were quickly sent home. NotPetya, however, continued to wreak havoc, spreading across several multinational companies, virtually shutting down the Ukrainian government and resulting in over $10 billion USD in damages total.

Because of that attack, Maersk's entire business shut down, and warehouses and terminals across the world were left in chaos, with no way to find out any information about current cargo. They were dead in the water.

What's more, as they began to recover from the attack, they realised that although they'd made back-ups of all of their individual servers, they had no back-up for the most important part of their network – the domain controllers, which formed the secure map of the rest of the network, and which would allow them to get the rest of the network working.

It took ten days – and finding one lone surviving domain controller in Ghana – to get most of the company running again. It took two months to make a full recovery. Estimates of total losses go anywhere from $250 million USD up, while many logistics companies whose livelihoods depended on Maersk also saw huge losses.

And Maersk weren't the only ones hit hard. Since surfacing in 2016, NotPeyta (and its earlier variant Peyta) wreaked havoc on Ukraine's Chernobyl Nuclear Power Plant monitoring system; German DHL, the Cadbury factory in Tasmania, and FedEx. American brand Mondelez International (who helm Oreo and Cadbury, among others) have had their clean-up insurance claim rejected on the grounds that NotPeyta is an 'act of war'.

You'll be pleased to know the maker of NotPeyta was eventually fined and arrested. But it's only a matter of time before another attack. NotPetya was a huge wake up call for organisations across the world, and there's no doubt that a similar attack could – and probably will – happen again. Large multinationals have taken note. Many of them have significantly upped their security and now have far greater plans in place to protect against attacks and enable them to recover should their systems be compromised. But when it comes to smaller companies, we still have a lot to learn.

* * *

Patch management
Acquiring, testing, and installing multiple 'patches' or code changes, within an administered computer system.
Imagine your computer system like a bucket – when it springs a leak, you need a patch to protect everything in the bucket. But those patches are also the most vulnerable parts of your bucket (or computer system), so keeping on top of them is vital!

* * *

CYBERATTACKS ON A SMALLER SCALE

You might be wondering what Maersk has to do with small businesses. You may even have been reading that story and thinking, 'It's okay, we're just small – no-one would attack us.' Unfortunately, that's not the case.

According to one report, 43% of cyberattack victims in 2019 were small businesses. Smaller businesses are often easier to hack into, have more lax security systems, and may have connections to larger companies that allow cyber criminals to then attack larger organisations. Just this happened when US retailer Target was hacked by infiltrating a small HVAC company with access credentials to Target's network.

Cybersecurity issues are doing more than just damaging big companies. The rise of ransomware and compromised emails is seeing businesses have their payroll stolen, their data hacked into, and customer details leaked. That kind of challenge could sink a small company – both due to loss of income and reputation or increased costs.

Much can be forgiven, but if you lose a customer's data, it's often game over.

While that's important on an individual company level, it's also important for us as a nation. After all, Aotearoa New Zealand runs on small businesses. A third of Kiwis are employed by organisations with fewer than 20 employees, and some 97% of the businesses within Aotearoa are small businesses.

For us to grow as a country, we need to encourage and support people with great ideas who want to accomplish something big. But to do that, we have to protect them, their ideas, and their businesses. We have to stay safe. That's where cybersecurity comes in. Cybersecurity gives businesses the confidence that they can safely invest in their innovation and in their growth – and because of that, it's pretty much key to growing Aotearoa New Zealand (I know, big claim!).

Cyberattacks, phishing, spam, ransomware… Cybersecurity might all seem frightening – but luckily, it doesn't have to be. It is entirely possible to protect your business and your data from attacks.

This book will show you how.

WHAT TO EXPECT FROM THIS BOOK

Within these pages, you'll find more IT terms than you probably ever needed to know in your life – but you'll also discover easy-to-understand explanations of them in break out boxes throughout.

You'll find explanations of the biggest threats facing Kiwi businesses – and you'll learn how you can protect your own business from them.

You'll find stories of Kiwi businesses who have been hacked, scammed, or compromised – and you'll hear stories of how they've overcome these challenges and protected themselves.

You'll find explanations of all the most common scams and other information that might make you nervous – and you'll find the tools and advice you need to make sure your business is secure.

You'll learn how your team can be the weak link in your security – and you'll get a guide for engaging them in cybersecurity and turning them into your best line of defence.

I can't promise I won't freak you out or make you seriously worried about how secure your business is – but I can promise that I'll show you what to do about it. Too many Kiwi businesses aren't doing the minimum to secure their IT and data – but cybersecurity is vital to a successful, sustainable business, and I'm all about helping businesses thrive.

WHY SHOULD YOU LISTEN TO ME?

But what do I know? Why on earth should you pay any attention to a Kiwi bloke with a couple of kids and a passion for long-distance swimming?

Well, I've been in this business since the early days – back before IT was even a career. From working in a third-party network fault management business and gaining exposure to the coolest (at-the-time) new technologies like green screen terminals, through to my time in the UK contracting to a professional services company, I've always had a passion for understanding the latest technologies. I gained years of experience in troubleshooting on massive networks and acquired virtually every system qualification you can possibly imagine.

Along the way, I also joined the Territorials as a combat engineer, rising to the rank of Troop Sergeant. I learned the values of discipline, attention to detail, and leading and training teams with a singular focus on the mission whilst maintaining situational awareness. I also gained a true understanding of what the word 'security' means.

After returning to New Zealand nearly twenty years ago, I worked across computing and IT security companies and realised that small businesses here were all facing virtually the same IT issues. Most didn't have huge network requirements (in fact, the majority could make do with a single Cisco 800 Series router), however, most systems engineers were blithely unaware of network security principles so clients were ending up with misconfigured routers and unsecure network perimeters on a routine basis.

When the opportunity came up to run my own business, it seemed like a no-brainer – I'd get the chance to affect real change in New Zealand businesses and protect them from all those 'bad guys' out there through responsive IT expertise.

I started to build a general IT business over time, and soon realised that cybersecurity was the number one threat facing businesses in today's world. By the mid-2010s, I was seeing ransomware attacks and phishing everywhere. The more I saw, the more I realised it would just get worse. These days, we start with a comprehensive security stack as our base offering at Vertech – because if we can't keep a business safe, there's no point in doing anything else.

We've made it our mission to help Kiwi businesses get guaranteed cybersecurity – and this book is just another step along the way.

SO WHO IS THIS BOOK FOR?

Cybersecurity affects all of us, but in different ways. I've specifically put this book together for small business owners on the lookout for how to protect their business. You've worked hard and have built a profitable business that supports a number of staff – you don't want to lose that. It can be hard when you feel like you can't control aspects of your business – especially when that aspect is something that could sink you.

I'd love this book to become your new cybersecurity bible: the book you turn to when you're not sure if you're doing things right; the book you take to your existing IT provider to ask them why the hell they're not doing the things you've learned from it; the book that will help you feel safe and protected once you (or a cybersecurity expert) have implemented the learnings from it.

So let's dive in – and get started on your journey to having a super-secure business.

1

AN INTRO TO CYBERSECURITY

NOW THAT YOU KNOW HOW CYBERSECURITY IMPACTS BUSINESSES, it's time to dig into the details of what it actually is and how you can keep your business safe.

So, what does cybersecurity actually encompass?

The dictionary might class it as the state of being protected against the criminal or unauthorised use of electronic data, or the measures taken to achieve this, but it encompasses so much more.

Essentially, cybersecurity is any and all tools and activities that protect you against a huge raft of cyberattacks, including:

Phishing
The most common form of cyber-attack. You receive what look like emails from reputable sources but are actually fraudulent. The goal is usually to trick you into installing malware or to steal sensitive data like credit card numbers and logins.

* * *

Ransomware
One of the biggest threats to small businesses, this is a type of malicious software designed to extort money by blocking access to your files or computer system until the ransom is paid. Unfortunately, just because you pay doesn't mean you'll get access back either.

* * *

Malware
Short for malicious software, this is a type of programme designed to gain access to your computer and/or cause damage to it. This could include computer viruses, worms, Trojan horses, or spyware. A rootkit back door to your system to allow further attacks may be deployed.

* * *

Social engineering
A tactic used to trick you into revealing sensitive information, making a monetary payment, or allowing access to your confidential data. Social engineering can be combined with any of the threats listed here to make you more likely to click on links, download malware, or trust a malicious source such that you send them confidential information.

* * *

Man-in-the-middle
Also known as an 'eavesdropping attack', this is when someone intercepts and relays messages between two people who believe they are interacting with one another. Once they're in the conversation, they can filter, manipulate, and steal sensitive information. This can be via network-based sniffing attacks or

more complicated internet redirection attacks on internet infrastructure.

* * *

Distributed denial-of-service (DDoS)

A bombardment and overload of an organisation's central server with simultaneous data requests. Multiple compromised systems are used to generate these data requests. A DDoS attack aims to stop the server from fulfilling legitimate requests, providing a situation for criminal hackers to extort the victim for money. For example, the August 2020 attacks against the New Zealand Stock Exchange.

* * *

Structured query language injection (SQL)

During programming, an attacker will insert malicious code into a web server that uses SQL, the standard language for relational database management systems. An SQL injection makes the poorly protected server reveal sensitive information.

* * *

Zero-day exploit

When a network or system vulnerability is announced, there is a window of time before a patch or solution is used to fix the issue. Within that timeframe, cyber attackers will exploit the vulnerability. Some exploits have been found to be Nation State Espionage tools leaked into the dark web!

* * *

Cross-site scripting (XSS)

Similar to an SQL injection, this involves injecting malicious code into a website. In this case, though, the malicious code runs only in the user's browser when they visit the attacked website, and it goes after the visitor directly, not the website. Used to harvest credit card information from websites by exploiting URL vulnerabilities.

* * *

Credential reuse

An attack that takes advantage of people using the same password multiple times. Once attackers have a collection of usernames and passwords from a breached website or service (easily acquired on any number of black market websites on the internet), they know that if they use these same credentials on other websites there's a chance they'll be able to log in.

* * *

Think of it like your home. New Zealand is a very safe place to live overall – in most neighbourhoods you could accidentally leave your door unlocked and you'd come home hours later to find nothing changed (except perhaps the bird your cat has dragged in ...).

However, when it comes to the internet, your house isn't in a nice neighbourhood. In fact, there aren't any nice neighbour-hoods. Wherever you set up shop, you're always only across the fence from a bad guy. In fact, every bad guy on the planet lives on the same street. All day, every day those bad guys are rattling your windows and trying your door handles, just to see if they can get in. They may not have gotten in yet, but it's only a matter of time.

This is the nature of cyberattacks. They're impersonal, oppor-tunistic and mostly automated, trying every house they can until they find a cracked-open window or an unlocked door. With a tool like ZMAP on my laptop & a Gigabit internet connection I can scan the entire internet (4.3 billion IP addresses) in less than an hour!

Now, these cyberattacks are not something that happen just once – they're happening every day to hundreds and thousands of businesses and individuals, perpetrated by attackers all over the world. Sometimes I'll have a look at the logs of our clients' firewalls and see how they change throughout a day. Virtually every time I check, the logs look like a window on a winter's day – there's pretty much a constant drizzle of attacks raining down.

If you've got good security systems in place and a good IT provider, that drizzle shouldn't ever hit you. If you don't have a good system and provider, chances are at some point that rain is going to get through the cracks in your home and cause serious damage.

So, what are the weaknesses that are letting these bad guys through? Where are the cracks that are letting drizzle leak in to cause long-term damage?

THE MISTAKES WE'RE MAKING

Technology is more affordable and accessible than it's ever been. Whatever you need is only a few clicks away, whether it's a product or a service. But there are still many small businesses that cheap out on their technology and IT solutions. They just don't want to commit to quality hardware, software, security, or backups – the list goes on. They go for the cheapest solutions, which often means they spend nothing at all. They don't commit to reliable security or current software. They're setting them-selves, and their customers, up for disaster.

The question is, are you setting your own business up for disaster? Let's look at the four biggest mistakes people are making when it comes to cybersecurity:

MISTAKE #1: YOU AREN'T BACKING UP DATA.

As convenient as it is to have all your business's information in one place – such as a single local server or even a desktop PC – you're toast if anything happens to that hardware. For one, if you're lacking in IT security, you're making a cybercriminal's job easier. And two, if that hardware fails (as hardware eventually does; there's no way around this), you're left scrambling to recover your data and hope it's still accessible.

You should never risk your business like this, considering how easy it is to back up your business's data. You can back up data on-site, get a cloud-based service, or you can do both. The point is, you need to back up everything so you're ready should anything go wrong.

We'll take a look at how to ensure your business can continue without interruption should you get attacked in Chapter Five.

MISTAKE #2: YOU AREN'T KEEPING UP WITH THE TIMES.

Speaking of keeping things updated, when was the last time you updated your software? Developers are constantly fixing bugs, patching software, and improving usability. Skipping updates can leave you vulnerable. In early 2020, Cisco's Series 1001-X router was found to have a fatal flaw that potentially gave hackers network access – and access to connected devices.

This isn't the first router to have this kind of flaw and it won't be the last. Cisco pushed out an update to fix the flaw, but the update is useless if you don't install it.

Updates don't just apply to software; they apply to hardware as well. Anyone who's held onto a smartphone for too long knows that it gets slow, unresponsive and increasingly unable to handle basic tasks as it ages and tries to run newer and increasingly taxing programs. Over time, hardware performance degrades. Plus, the older your hardware is, the less compatible it is with current software. After a certain point, you can't update it anymore. Not only does that put you at risk of having unpatched (or unpatchable) flaws exploited, but old hardware is more likely to fail – taking your data with it.

You don't have to invest in new hardware every year or two, but keeping up with the times keeps you on top of your game.

MISTAKE #3: YOU DON'T TRAIN YOUR TEAM.

While most businesses hire smart people, you can't assume they know everything about the software you use – even if they've used it before. Your business might use a certain customer relationship management (CRM) application in a very specific way, so proper training on your systems ensures everyone is on the same page – and that they are using the software to its (and their) greatest potential.

More than software training, your team also needs to be trained up on IT security and what part they can play in ensuring you have robust and reliable cybersecurity. They need to know the risks and how to keep your data secure. They need to know how to lock the door and check the windows. And they need to know what to do when it goes pear-shaped.

Never assume your team knows about the latest threats to small business – or that they even understand the basics of safe web browsing, for that matter. While you need to have IT security in place protecting your network, servers, data and so on, you also need to make sure your team understands that security and the threats that are out there. Your team should be aware of the consequences if any data becomes compromised. I'll take a look at how you can engage your team in cybersecurity in more depth in Chapter Three of this book.

MISTAKE #4: YOU SKIP DATA SECURITY.

Data breaches happen every day, and most of them go unreported. You only hear about the biggest breaches on TV or online, and while major companies like Target or Facebook can recover from a data breach (as they have a lot of money to throw at the problem), most small businesses can't.

If you're lacking in IT security, you're putting sensitive data at risk. And that's not just proprietary business data, but also the personal and financial records of your customers.

It can mean the end of your business if credit card numbers, names, addresses, or phone numbers fall into the wrong hands. Customers will no longer trust you.

Your own employees likely won't trust you either, especially if their personal data is on the line, not to mention their reputation. Keeping your data secure is absolutely vital to protecting your business – and your people.

ARE YOU BEING SERVER-ED?

When it comes to your cybersecurity, your server is possibly your most important asset. I've already mentioned servers – both physical and 'the cloud' – as ways to back up and handle your business's data.

I know that a lot of people aren't sure what the difference is, or which way to go.

So, who's more at risk of cyberattacks – and how do you pick which one is right for your business?

* * *

Server
A dedicated computer or device on a network that is designed to process requests and deliver data to another computer. Different types of servers do different jobs, from delivering email and video to protecting internal networks and hosting websites. They're basically the beating heart of a system, managing all your network resources.

* * *

Twenty years ago, just about everyone had physical servers. You'd have a room or a closet that powered your whole network of computers, and if anything happened to one of your physical servers, you'd pretty much be screwed. If you were sensible, you'd have your networks under lock and key, have back-ups for days, and have strict policies about who could access what. If you were less sensible, it was pretty easy for someone to walk in, gain access to your servers, and corrupt all your data and systems.

These days, there's another option – the cloud. Since it started gaining in popularity a little over a decade ago, it's become the go-to option for SMEs for both their systems and their data. And for good reason – it's easy to use, frees up the processing power of your computers, and often has a lower entry price point.

But, like all IT, there are some risks involved – not least because in this case, you're storing your data on somebody else's physical servers, possibly in another part of the world.

What's more, cloud computing hasn't completely overtaken the need for physical, in-house servers. There's still a place for both – and both have their upsides. So how do you know whether to choose a physical server or the cloud from a cyberse-curity perspective? Let's take a look at the pros and cons:

PHYSICAL SERVER

Pros

- May be more cost effective long-term if you have a need for big processing power (i.e. you have lots of employees or run difficult processes through your systems) – you can budget any upgrades across several years.
- Easy to make physical back-ups.

- You 100% own it.

Cons

- High entry point cost-wise (you need all the physical equipment, including an air-conditioned room to keep all the equipment in).
- You're responsible for all updates and security.
- Someone could literally walk into your building and plug themselves into your server to access everything.

THE CLOUD

Pros

- Lower entry point cost-wise – normally a monthly cost per user.
- You don't need to worry about having local services (e.g. power, air conditioning, a rack).
- Most big providers have high levels of cybersecurity in place.
- Supports a more flexible kind of working, with your people able to access your information and systems from anywhere.
- Many tools will do up-to-the-minute back-ups regularly (but not all – see below!)

Cons

- You're not just magically storing your data in the actual clouds – all that cloud computing means is that you're storing your data on someone else's (much bigger) servers. That means you're completely reliant on them having the security needed to prevent any breaches.

- Many simply provide file synchronisation, not an actual back-up – if someone deletes a file, you may not be able to get it back.
- Can be slow depending on the power of their servers, bandwidth and their distance from you on the internet.

According to the National Cyber Security Alliance, 70 percent of cybercriminals are specifically out there targeting small businesses – yet despite that, small business owners often ignore the issue of cybersecurity. It's no surprise really, given it's the kind of problem that's so complicated that it can be tempting to sweep it under the rug.

As breach tactics become more sophisticated, so do the software and methodologies designed to keep out criminals. In a world far removed from the days when buying a product and installing it into your network was enough, it's easy to become overwhelmed by the complexity and breakneck pace of advancing cybersecurity best practices.

Our biases make the possibility of a hack seem remote, while our limited resources make the cost of protection appear too high to even consider. However, the first step to getting savvy is to accept that cyberattack isn't some unlikely crisis, but a virtual inevitability. It's a tough pill to swallow, but leaving it to chance is like flipping a coin where a 'tails' outcome results in your business shutting for good.

Whether you choose physical servers or the cloud, it's vital that you make cybersecurity a key part of your decision making. But how can you protect your little corner of the world?

It's all about moving into a safer environment – challenging your assumptions about what will make you safer and ensuring that you're covering all possible entrances into your technology. In the next chapter, we'll dig into your cybersecurity basics – the things that, if you have them in place, will ensure that you'll be far more protected than the majority of businesses.

A CLOSER LOOK: EDENFX'S CYBERSECURITY STRATEGY

Trans-Tasman edenfx HSE is a recruitment company that specialises in quietly sourcing excellent personnel for roles in health, safety, environmental, quality and risk (HSEQR).

With a lot of critical client and personnel info in their possession, and a need to keep operations moving at all times, edenfx understand how important it is to keep vulnerabilities in check. So, after a real hammering, they knew they had to up their game.

A FAST-MOVING COMPANY – AND INCREASING IT VULNERABILITIES

When they started, their small business server at their HQ in Silverdale, Auckland was more than enough to handle their requirements. Since launching in 2008, edenfx has gone from a team of two to 22, and now help thousands of talented Kiwis and Aussies find the right roles in construction, HR and health and safety. Great news for their company – but their IT services struggled to keep pace. And when hardware gets old, it's prone to failure.

Unfortunately, that's just what happened a couple of years ago. Thankfully, their IT specialist – a well-meaning one-man band who'd been working with them since day dot – was able to restore the server from a backup and onto loan equipment while he got up to speed. But here things started to unravel.

In the process of restoring data, the IT guy unwisely opened a remote desktop protocol (RDP) to the recovery server, ostensibly to monitor the process overnight. But here's the catch: there were vulnerabilities in the RDP that enabled an attacker to encrypt the server.

Within a week they were ransomwared. Which they restored from backup, again.

A few days later, they were ransomwared again. Three major strikes.

DOWNTIME COSTS MORE THAN TIME ALONE

A hardware failure and restore of this nature costs a company like edenfx about a week. Anyone who's been in business knows that a week without your data is a serious pain.

Firstly there's the initial hit of frustration from the downtime itself, and the efforts to contain the damage. But as an outage extends to days at a time, there's also the 22 staff that aren't able to work to anything near their usual capacity – with salaries going nowhere, and no real revenue coming in.

That cost extends to reputation, too, since they're having to deal with clients and business partners calling up and getting the same dead-end answer of yes, we're still down.

At this point, edenfx thought it was a good time to upgrade their IT specialists. And the one-man band agreed!

GROWING THEIR IT WITH THE COMPANY

One of the most rewarding parts about working with other businesses is seeing how they grow and develop, and in being able to grow with them. You want to provide them with those scalable, resilient and reliable solutions that meet their needs. I don't want to have nightmares about them losing their data – and nor should they!

When edenfx jumped on board with us at Vertech, the first thing we did was to explore their wants and needs to make sure they were going to get the kinds of scalable solutions that would keep their data – and their reputation – safe.

We transitioned them off their server entirely. Most small businesses don't need a server at all, which is why a cloud-based operation was their best solution going forward. It would mean their data would be more secure and just as accessible by their internal teams.

They also implemented a full security stack (something we'll cover later in this book) and we organised a full support plan which means they can call us about every little thing that might worry them and we'll get it sorted for them. We're proactively working together to look at what they need and guarantee their safety. They get the service they need, when they need it, and now they've got better peace of mind – and so do we for them!

2

CYBERSECURITY BASICS

WHEN I STARTED VERTECH IN 2010, we tended to be driven by our clients – we let them decide which antivirus software they wanted, whether they wanted spam filtering, and other tools like web filtering that we'd recommend. They didn't have to have them, if they chose not to.

Typically, they tended to choose the bare minimum and the cheapest option available. They thought that your off-the-shelf antivirus software would do the job. To me, that seems a bit backwards. You're trying to protect your systems, your data, your business and your reputation. So why would you choose something that might not do the job, or just one or two pieces of basic protection when there's so much at stake?

Over time it became clear that having just one or two weapons in your digital security arsenal just isn't enough, and it really didn't work trying to defend our clients using tools selected according to the lowest bid!

I'm in the New Zealand Defence Force Army Reserve as a Sergeant of Engineers. A century ago, armies across the world re-introduced the steel helmet – pretty much the first piece of body armour for soldiers since the invention of the rifle bullet – because there were a huge number of injuries due to the modern artillery shrapnel shell. Today, when soldiers go out on missions, they'll layer up with protection: a modern Kevlar helmet, body armour, ceramic plates fore and aft. As Engineers, we have additional protective equipment such as MOPP (Mission Oriented Protective Posture) suits for situations where we need protection from biological, chemical, nuclear or radiological threats. We now drive in armoured vehicle convoys protected by Radio Controlled IED Jammers to defeat roadside bombers. The old 'Battle Bowler' alone just doesn't cut it anymore.

In the same way, neither will antivirus software alone protect your business. Just as we layer up in the army, your business needs a number of levels of defence if you want to truly protect your data, your technology, and your people.

When it comes to cybersecurity, there's a lot to think about. Today's threats are a lot larger and more diverse than people expect. Times, technologies, and threats change quickly, and it can be easy to fall behind, or feel safe when things are apparently running smoothly.

How I like to describe the situation is by reminding people that you live a zero distance from every bad guy on the planet – they're the ones checking to see which doors and windows you've left open. Someone out there right now is trying to access your bank records, hack your phone, spy through your laptop's camera. So, if you don't have someone watching out for your network, you're going to get hit. It's just a matter of time.

No one's too clever or too safe to be taken advantage of by a cyber-attack, and it's often the ones who think they're smart enough that are the first to fall victim. If you think you'll spot it before it happens, then you'll miss the cleverest attacks that bypass your personal filter.

The thing is, cybersecurity attacks aren't personal. Hackers, malware, and viruses don't discriminate and aren't going specifically for your data because it's you. They just look around, find weaknesses and exploit them. It's done on a massive scale, it's automated, and it's completely anonymous.

If we take a look at your typical firewall stats and logs and the spam filtering stats, it becomes pretty clear that cyberattacks are a constant problem. Someone's always trying to scale your fence and sneak past the dogs. There are new threats and vulnerabilities coming out all the time, and you've got to be vigilant to clear them out.

Getting your cybersecurity basics covered is like putting up a solid fence all the way round the property (not just the front!), installing an effective security alarm system, putting a deadbolt on the doors and windows, and making sure the security dogs are patrolling. You've got to have a coordinated approach that layers up protections across all levels.

It's a simple enough strategy but one we see too many businesses ignoring. And it's easy to ignore if you haven't yet suffered an attack or your current security is silently holding back the worst of the damage. We don't tend to hear much about how prevention works, but it does work. And we know that there are more than enough horror stories of businesses losing precious information – and more importantly, losing trust from their clients – due to a data breach.

In the military, when we plan to execute a mission, we consider the most likely enemy action and the most dangerous course of enemy action. We turn the problem around and look at it from different points of view and what-if scenarios, putting control measures in place to ensure that we have a good outcome and the mission succeeds. In contemporary army combat engineering, we'll have guys in front of the infantry, with trucks sweeping the ground looking for mines, command wires and other threats.

At Vertech IT Services, our clients expect us to keep them secure, sweeping the ground ahead of them to keep them safe and providing the layers of protection they need. We make sure that they can get through and do their mission well and that they can move forward with confidence.

There are eight essential layers that you need to have in place for your business. Let's look at them from the outside in:

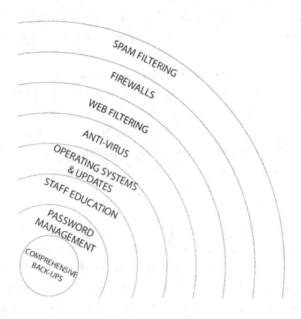

SPAM FILTERING

About 70% of your computer and network infections happen because spam gets through – and because somebody clicked on something they shouldn't have.

* * *

Spam
Irrelevant or unsolicited messages, usually for advertising, phishing, or spreading viruses. The name came about after the Monty Python 'Spam' sketch from 1970 where the word's uttered at least 132 times, appearing in every menu item at a café. Nowadays, to be 'spammed' is to be inundated with excessive postings or irrelevant material – mostly the irritating,

impersonal emails sent to everyone and no one, typically in the hopes of gaining your information (phishing).

* * *

A spam filter is the security at the door. It assesses your emails and checks whether they meet certain criteria. If it detects unsolicited and unwanted emails, it'll stop them from getting to your inbox (often re-directing them to a quarantined 'Spam' folder).

Clicking links in spam messages often opens the door directly to malware that then infects your computer or network. That's why spam filtering is a critical aspect of a cybersecurity toolkit. It helps prevent users clicking on dubious links and exposing your network to potentially harmful content.

The size of the mesh

Some spam filters will prevent unsolicited emails from reaching your inbox by checking the sender address against your contacts or a blacklist. Others will read the content of an email or the subject line before it reaches you and determine if the content is relevant.

What kind of spam filter you use to keep your inbox tidy and your network safe will depend on what you need. Content-based or header filters will help reduce newsletters, ads, and sales emails cluttering your inboxes, while a permissions-based filter or challenge-response filter will sort senders based on codes or approval. What's relevant and useful to you and your business needs to be the yardstick here.

It's worth noting that some email platforms have spam filters built in. Gmail and Outlook have such a tight filter that the odd normal email gets sorted into spam. The webmail of a small operator, however, will be less likely to have the infrastructure or resources to achieve the same, so you need to layer it with other filters and checks.

Promises, promises

Spam messages often famously promise performance enhancement pills cheaply and discretely, large sums of cash in exchange for help, or international romance (so-called 'honey trapping'). All they are is a vehicle to collect your data and exploit you. Spam often tricks the vulnerable and the naïve with something that sounds too good to be true – and most certainly is.

There's a new, sophisticated email scam you need to watch out for called Sextortion.

The victim will receive an email claiming that a virus was installed on a porn website which recorded them through their webcam. What then follows is extortion and threats of exposure. They'll claim that their software has collected the victim's contacts from messengers, e-mails and social networks, and if they don't receive Bitcoins or another difficult-to-track digital currency, then they'll send a video of the victim to all their contacts.

It's a play on shame, the fear of tainting your professional image – and using that fear to drive a poor decision. We have seen it increasing in frequency and it's often made more effective by combining the email with a known database of exposed email addresses & passwords.

If this – or any other type of scam email – makes it through the spam filters and into your inbox, simply delete the message (and/or click the 'Phish Alert' button). Do not click on any links, and do not reply. Do not download any software to check your computer for viruses but follow procedures to report these types of criminal emails.

Remember: 'Think Before You Click' is more important than ever these days. Educating your staff and giving them some basic cybersecurity training is essential as a last line of defence in your business. We'll explore this further in Chapter Three of this book.

FIREWALLS

The next layer is your firewall.

* * *

Firewall
A network security layer that monitors the incoming and outgoing network data – what goes between you and the internet – and permits or blocks data depending on a set of rules.

* * *

The term 'firewall' pre-dates computers, and still refers to fire-resistant barriers used to prevent the spread of fire through buildings, around electrical substations, and in cars. In principle, it's the same idea: a break between you and risk.

The basic firewall types

There are three kinds of firewalls used by companies to protect their data and their network – and then there's UTM. Let's look at each:

* * *

Packet Filters
These control network access by analysing the outgoing and incoming data packets, allowing or blocking data by checking it against known criteria (such as acceptable IP addresses, packet types, port numbers etc.). This type is good for small networks, though can't handle stronger attacks.

* * *

Stateful Inspection (SPI)
Sometimes called 'dynamic packet filtering', SPI examines traffic

streams end to end. It's a powerful firewall architecture that analyses and inspects the validity of your connections. Much more secure than packet filters alone, and best used at the network layer in the OSI model.

* * *

Proxy Server Firewalls

Also called 'application level gateways', these are the most secure type of firewall since they protect the network's resources by filtering messages at the application layer. They'll do a great job of masking your IP address and limiting traffic types, providing complete and protocol-aware security analysis for the protocols they support. They're by far the most robust type of firewall and can give you improved network performance.

* * *

Not all firewalls are created equal, though, and if you want a next-generation firewall, then you'll need something more powerful than the one you get with the free router from your ISP (probably a simple packet filter).

Truth be told, if you're in business, it's definitely worth spending a few extra hundred dollars and getting a proper next-gen firewall with a security subscription in place. It'll take a clear look at the traffic going through the firewall and disregard or dispose of anything untoward. That's where you need an Urchin Tracking Module (UTM).

UTMs

Simply put, a UTM is a firewall on steroids. The free router from your ISP is going to have some pretty basic firewall functionality, which may be okay for the casual at-home user. It'll stop the outside world getting in, and will allow pretty much everything outbound.

We install UTMs for our clients to safeguard and inspect the larger and more sensitive scale of traffic that's going out of their organisation. If you've got a company of any size, you really should be looking at a UTM, because one of the most significant threats to business operations is ransomware.

If someone on the network (a well-meaning colleague) clicks on an email that perhaps they should have avoided, this could initiate a ransomware attack. The attack will send a request for an encryption key from its own command control server somewhere out there on the internet. That server is going to try and send back its encryption key, which will then start blocking all your files – and then you're up a certain creek without a certain paddle.

The UTM looks into the packets of data going out and checks them against a security subscription that can tell it who and where the dodgy places are. The UTM does a bunch of other things but that's the part I love.

When I'm out there trying to protect my clients, I've got to have a UTM in place.

WEB FILTERING

If you're not protecting and policing what your staff are doing, then you're going to be losing money one way or the other – especially from accidentally going to malicious sites or having compromised ad injections coming in and taking advantage of vulnerabilities in your operating systems.

Web filters
Sometimes known as 'content control software', these allow or block which websites or parts of a website a user can visit. It's not uncommon to see this on school computers and work networks, preventing sites that are deemed inappropriate or 'not safe for work'.

* * *

But it's not just blocking sites wholesale, which is something that can be easily done through the firewall. Websites nowadays have content aggregated from across the internet, so a web filter needs to check not just the site's domain but block out dangerous content – and stop access to time-draining sites like Facebook or Reddit.

Web filtering strengthens your network's cybersecurity by being a first line of defence against malware and attacks. There's always a good chance that someone might fall for clickbait or accidentally engage with a pop-up, which is why blacklisting malicious websites and harmful material on trusted pages is a basic first step. Like with spam filters, the web filters can either block content entirely, or re-direct the user to a safe quarantine page to let them know where and how they've stepped wrong.

Get onto it

Web filters improve productivity. Sure, a ten-minute browse through TradeMe or Facebook when it's quiet might be harmless, but those 10 minutes a day, five days a week rack up to the equivalent of a 40-hour working week by the end of the year per person. If you have 15 staff paid $25 per hour, that's over $15,000 per year going out the door without any productive returns.

A web filter can deny access to those common distractions like social media or shopping – something that your staff should be welcome to do on their own time, such as lunch breaks, or on their own devices. The right filtering solution can even make this possible by allocating windows for use during breaks, which can be an attractive compromise. But do keep in mind that your social media manager probably should have access to Facebook, even if the rest of the company doesn't. Adjust and filter according to your team's roles.

Improve your bandwidth – and your reputation

Some careful filtering will also improve your network's efficiency by freeing up the bandwidth that tends to disappear with video and audio streaming. Spotify and YouTube can be fun, but they're data hungry. Set limits on sites that slow your company's overall network so you can reserve the bandwidth for more critical things like VoIP or accounting software – these things shouldn't take second stage to someone's latest playlist.

Then there are the legal aspects. If an employee uses the company network to illegally download or access a risky site (think illegal, racist, or pornographic content), then you could be responsible for violating copyright law and/or risk your business's reputation.

But what to block?

Your policies and approaches are going to vary, but here's a common shortlist on what your filters could prevent:

- Certain social media sites, such as Facebook. Unless you're the social media manager, you probably spend too much time on here already.
- Certain topics, such as sports or celebrity gossip. If your team talk a lot about cricket, then you'll notice the drop in productivity every time there's a test match.
- The sending of discriminatory or threatening messages. This can damage your business's reputation overnight, so better to nip it in the bud. It also helps to teach your staff to conduct themselves as if one day anyone could see their entire computer, email and web history – so they'd be better not to put their foot in it.
- Using company resources for personal gain. This could include using work computers for personal emails or to create and print flyers for a dance class.
- Online betting, gambling, shopping and auction sites, and games. None of which have anything to do with work and, unless you've specifically instructed a team member to look up secondhand office furniture, aren't worth the company's productivity. Save it for lunch.

- Obscene material. Porn and other graphic content is considered 'not safe for work' for good reason. Beyond the HR issues it raises, there is serious potential to damage your business's reputation.
- Downloading large/non-work files (including copyrighted material). Not only does this sponge up your bandwidth, but there's those legal risks associated with piracy that your company is better to avoid.

Once you know what you're going to block or limit, it's simply a matter of implementing the filter when and how you'd like. But it's far from set-and-forget. Like all cybersecurity, it's an ongoing and evolving process that requires some proactivity and monitoring to ensure you're getting the best out of your bandwidth and your team.

* * *

Antivirus software
Programmes that scan and protect computers from malware, spyware, and other hostile attempts to take, remove, or ransom your data. It's the equivalent of the immune system to the human body – it checks, detects, and eliminates.

* * *

ANTIVIRUS & ENDPOINT PROTECTION

You might think that the antivirus software that came as part of a computer bundle is going to be enough to keep the bad guys at bay, but that's rarely the case. The problem is that there are more antivirus solutions out there than there are makes of cars.

You'll definitely want to start with something like your classic signature-based antivirus software, but these days this is simply not enough to protect you adequately. Cyberattacks are becoming more powerful and malware more sophisticated – malware is often sold now with advanced obfuscation techniques such as changing, 'polymorphic' code, for instance – so the reality is that your current antivirus software probably doesn't cut it anymore. You're going to need endpoint protection, too.

Endpoint protection

Endpoint protection software utilises machine learning and artificial intelligence to detect, prevent, and respond to changing threats as they occur. It takes some of the classic ideas of cybersecurity – antivirus software, malware security, detection and response to threats, device management – and takes these to the next level by utilising neural networks, software behavioural analysis and exploit protection with automatic recovery techniques. A next-generation antivirus with endpoint protection is completely autonomous and takes approaches like deep file inspection and behavioural analyses to identify the kinds of malware that behaves unlike people.

In Chapter One, we mentioned some of the common cyberattacks. An ideal antivirus will help protect you from everything on that list, from ransomware to phishing and malware, by recognising and blocking threats before they're a risk to your network.

But antivirus software also helps protect your other sensitive data, including the credit card details and passwords saved to your browser's auto-populating feature or your Apple Keychain. Just as a firewall can blacklist certain email links, antivirus software can double your email protection by filtering the Trojan horses and other viruses that sneak their way into your computer through innocent-looking pictures and links in emails.

One question that crops up is whether your off-the-shelf antivirus software is going to cut it. Well, it might cover you for the basics but probably won't include extra security features like financial transaction protection, digital file shredders, or program isolation. If you're thinking cybersecurity, then you'd be wise to expand your thoughts to malware, whitelisting application control, and even device control – after all, if there's no reason for users to plug in USB sticks, why let them?

Viruses don't just come from the internet or dodgy emails

The USB drive or device is a great way to transmit infections from place to place – in fact, pre-internet, viruses were transmitted via floppy drives, since these were the most common medium for file transfer. Since people's attention is more directed at internet security, they often forget how much we still rely on USB sticks and devices – and the risks they carry.

Nowadays, I expect pretty much everyone to either physically block their USB ports, and/or invest in antivirus software with USB scanning. Add to this some common-sense approaches and staff education (which we'll discuss soon): don't plug in any old USB stick, especially not ones you find on the ground. And if you're at a trade show and a rep offers you a drive of their files, just ask them to email you instead.

Schedule regular check-ups

If you have bought some retail anti-malware software and you're installing it across multiple computers in your organisation, then it really does need to be checked on a regular basis to ensure that:

— it is getting its updates and its license has not expired;

— that it actually is running; and

— whether it has been catching anything.

Of the various issues on a computer that can cause the anti-malware software to stop working, sometimes it's user-related (e.g. a staff member disables it because it's been interfering with another application), or it's because a piece of malware has got on board and has disabled it so it can sink its hooks in deeper! Our counter to this is to set monitored alerts on our clients' machines so we can spot these issues early.

At the end of the day, choose carefully. There are free antivirus programs, freeware with upgrades and paid commercial programs. Remember you get what you pay for. If it's free, then it will not have the best security update feeds or protection technologies.

In a world where a Day-Zero worm can cover the globe in 24 hours, do you really want to shell out for a product that is 90% effective against all known threats but can't protect you from the 90% of threats that are yet to be discovered?

OPERATING SYSTEMS AND UPDATES

Operating system (OS) updates and security updates are absolutely essential. You've got to keep your operating system up-to-date, because those changes and upgrades are, among other things, patching vulnerabilities and weak spots that were missed when the OS first launched.

* * *

Operating System
The infrastructure of your computer, managing your hardware, software and providing basic programs. Today, the market for personal and business computers is largely split between the operating systems from Microsoft and Apple.

* * *

Don't be running Windows XP. Even Windows 7 is getting a bit tired, and its support from Microsoft has ended. Windows 10 is a massive jump ahead from many security perspectives. And keep the updates up to date. This goes for more than the OS itself; update your applications too, because they're what are actually going to be attacked – whether it's a specially crafted PDF attachment in your email, or a drive-by web page script working on an exploit in your web browser.

It can be a bit annoying to have to step away from your

computer while it goes through another twenty minutes or two hours of updates to make your experience better, but without it, you're leaving the door open for hackers, malware and viruses to sneak in.

In 2017, the American multinational consumer credit agency Equifax suffered a colossal data breach. Social Security numbers (a bit like NZ's IRD numbers), birth dates and home addresses were exposed because hackers were able to exploit a known vulnerability in a web application. The real kicker? The security update to patch the flaw was available for two months before the attack – but the company didn't update the software. Equifax later came to a $575 million (USD) settlement with the Federal Trade Commission.

So, you're never too big or small to update your software. It doesn't need to be a hassle; that's why we create a policy for our clients that works for them on their schedule and monitor the results.

STAFF EDUCATION

One thing that often gets forgotten is your people. In fact, they're one of your strongest defences against cybercriminals. That's why awareness training is so important – something we'll dig into further in the next chapter.

Staff education is often forgotten or ignored, but, as we've seen, it's often simple user mistakes that can cost your business its data and integrity. At the end of the day, if something gets through the above layers (like the occasional spam making its way to your inbox) then your last layer of defence is the person sitting in front of their keyboard making the decision as to whether they should click a link or innocent-looking picture. And you want them to make the right decision.

Training needs to happen now – it's better to keep away from the edge than have an ambulance at the bottom of the cliff, after all.

Ask yourself the following questions:

— Do you – or your team – know what to do if they discover a cybersecurity threat within your organisation?

— Do you have a step-by-step guide or instructions to help them avoid threats?

— What do you do if you lose your mobile or laptop?

— What do you do if you accidentally click on a dodgy link?

— What do you do if you think someone's infiltrated your physical server?

— Would they question and report an unknown guy walking through your warehouse or working on a PC in your office?

These are all situations that your staff should be prepared for, so start having the conversation now.

PASSWORD MANAGEMENT

Truth be told, passwords and their management are a pain. One website might require letters and a symbol; another demands 14 characters; your bank needs 10, a four-digit pin, and your mother's maiden name. So it's easier to use the same three or four passwords for everything, right? After all, that's more secure than one password for everything.

Well, here's the problem with that strategy.

Let's assume you have a Gmail account, an Amazon account, a TradeMe account, a work and a personal account with Farmers and some others. You use the same password for all of those. And you use the same account details to order gift cards for your clients.

Now the gift card website's been hacked; the crooks get your credit card information and a list of all the users and their data. That list gets published or sold on the internet, and now your info is up for grabs. Someone's out there buying up with your credit card. Don't believe that this happens? Check out www.haveIbeenpwned.com.

Remember, all someone has to do is try your same login

information on one of a dozen popular sites and they have access to all your information. That's why you need to have different passwords for each and every application.

Make your life easier by getting a personal password management tool that will enable you to have one decent password that protects all your passwords and you can generate secure passwords for each of them.

A password manager lets you oversee and manage all your login credentials for all your devices securely. It's like a digital safe for your accounts – but it's also like a mint, generating unique, difficult-to-hack passwords so that you don't fall into the habit of using the same couple of passwords across your network. It'll do two things well, and has a hidden bonus:

— It makes every login more secure and avoids the risks of repeated passwords

— It means you can quickly and easily remove someone from all your systems as soon as they leave the business

— BONUS: It's a time saver!

A recent survey of 130,000 business owners by a US security company found that five percent of businesses rely on sticky notes on computers for their passwords. Another six percent have one password for everything – which is a great way to have all your accounts, profiles and information stolen in one fell swoop. Around 17 percent will use spreadsheets to track passwords, but even if they're password protected, it's not that difficult to crack.

The vast majority of businesses surveyed – around 60 percent – have no plan whatsoever. That might look like passwords written down in a black book that a receptionist or office manager keeps in their desk. I know this, because if I have to go looking for it then that's where I'll usually find it.

Passwords are fundamentally private, not public, things. Beyond your own passwords, consider all the passwords your team use in your business. Just recently I was on a couple of clients' sites and found out that most of them seemed to know each other's passwords. Now, if I had to do a forensic investigation (and track down who did what), I'd have no way of knowing who logged in to the computer and when. Not only does that have implications if you need to determine who was responsible for something (imagine a lawyer for the defence having fun with that!), it also means that staff will likely be able to access your accounts long after they've left the business. A password management tool for your whole team enables you to remove them as soon as they leave and keep your systems secure (although we often have to remind clients to tell us when this happens as sometimes it's weeks before they remember to remove an ex-employee!).

And the bonus? If you have a password management tool in place, the low cost of one of these tools is easily made up for in terms of time savings for your employees. At a typical $4 per person, if you can save the average worker just 10 minutes per month, it really pays for itself!

Multi-factor Authentication, or the 'One Time Password'

It's worth knowing about some extra resources for your passwords, like multi-factor authentication. Rather than just using your email and password to get access to your critical info, multi-factor authentication (sometimes called 'two-factor authentication' or '2FA') adds another step to ensure it's just you that has access.

It's common to see this technique used by SMEs to get access to certain banking info, for example, and is particularly useful for anyone who wants to access one account (say, their Gmail) but frequently changes machines on a network and doesn't want to be accidentally left logged in.

Multi-factor combines something you already know (like your PIN) with something you have (like an extra device, such as a phone or a dongle that delivers a unique number to you, or even your fingerprint). That way, even if someone has your login details, they're unlikely to be able to access your info without that extra feature.

Text message

Google has a feature where your registered phone number receives a text with a six-digit code if you want to log in to your Gmail from a new device. It's relatively straightforward, since most people have their phones with them constantly, and helps protect you whenever you change device.

Tokens or Dongle

Similar to the text message service, some banks issue tokens or dongles – keychain-sized devices that generate authentication data that forms the multi-factor login data. These could be disconnected (that is, they generate numbers alone), connected (like a USB that needs to be inserted/connected/swiped before you can get access), or software (like a security certificate on your device).

Location

This one's relatively new but becoming increasingly important as we move toward more remote working environments. It's essentially a combination of login details and password while you're on site, but if you're working from an off-site location, you'd then need the token to gain access.

COMPREHENSIVE BACK-UPS

Finally, comprehensive back-ups are the core of your cybersecurity. If something gets through all the above layers, then a robust back-up will ensure you keep running.

Losing data – your emails, files and servers – is probably the worst thing that can happen to a business. Not only can it impact the trust between you and your clients, it can also prevent you from continuing to operate. It's critical to have strong backups, to not rely on file synchronisation, and to test your back-ups regularly for functionality. And if all else fails, have a back-up plan. This is something we'll talk about more in detail in Chapter Five with 'Disaster Recovery'.

Whether you get stung with ransomware, or a user accidentally deletes an important file, or you suffer from equipment failure (like losing a device or hard drive), most people know that you have to have some form of back-up. But what kind of back-ups do you need?

I always operate on the 3-2-1 Rule that I talk about more in Chapter Five. It's simply this:

Keep 3 copies of any critical data

Use 2 different formats for data storage

Have 1 backup off site

The 3-2-1 Rule is going to save you a world of headaches should the worst happen.

A word of warning

Dropbox, Google Drive, OneDrive and the like aren't back-ups! They simply take your data and put it in the same format off-site. If you delete a file or suffer from a malware attack, the local will sync with the off-site version, and then both copies are encrypted.

Every passing hour of downtime costs your business. Comprehensive back-ups, and having a disaster recovery plan – the worst-case scenario recovery strategy – is what gets you back on track as soon as possible.

Cybersecurity Basics Checklist

Important! Like all checklists in this book, this is just a starting point. Our recommendation is that you engage with a professional IT firm to ensure that your cybersecurity meets your business's needs.

Spam filtering

☐ Implement a spam filter – it's better to get false positives than false negatives

☐ Make sure the quarantine does not include KNOWN bad email

Firewalls

☐ Install a UTM firewall with an active security subscription with alerts and egress filtering

☐ Enable Windows firewalls

Web filtering

☐ Engage a web filter to limit what sites and what content can be accessed

☐ Set time limits – all the time, or open up some doors at lunch, for example.

Choose what to block or limit for all or some of your team:

☐ Social media sites (e.g. Facebook, Instagram, Reddit)

☐ Certain topics (e.g. celebrities, movies, sports, travel)

☐ Discriminatory or threatening messages

☐ Company resources in general (e.g. print and software access)

☐ Online gambling and betting (e.g. poker sites, TAB)

☐ Online shopping and auction sites (e.g. Amazon, TradeMe, eBay)

☐ Porn and other graphic content (includes some image-hosting sites)

☐ Video and music streaming sites (e.g. YouTube, Spotify)

☐ Files over a certain size

☐ Piracy-enabling or illegal streaming sites

Antivirus

☐ Invest in professional next-generation endpoint protection software

☐ Block USB ports & unneeded devices if necessary

☐ Enable tamper protection

☐ Whitelist business programs, and remove local admin rights from staff

☐ Monitor the software to ensure it is running, getting updates and alerts if malware is found

Updates

☐ Ensure your operating system is up to date and secure

☐ Update programs when available and from reputable sites and sources

☐ Regularly check your external devices like printers and scanners for drivers and other software updates.

☐ Automate the process to happen at a time which maximises successful deployment and reduces disruption

Staff education

Educate your team on:

☐ How to spot spam and phishing. Remember – think before you click!

☐ Why and how web filtering is in place

☐ What antivirus software looks like, and how to prevent (i.e. no USB sticks)

☐ Check your computer for updates now

☐ Check your computer's update settings so that you get notifications when they're available

☐ Develop a cybersecurity plan, including a disaster recovery strategy (see Chapter Six)

☐ Plan for the loss of devices

☐ Check your operating system is up to date and secure

Passwords

☐ Educate staff on the importance of password privacy

☐ Remove the auto-fill passwords from your browser (e.g. Chrome)

☐ Have a professional IT specialist recommend a secure password tool and implement for your whole team

☐ Safely destroy the little black book of passwords and the spreadsheet – they're not safe!

Back-ups

☐ Prepare for failure now. Design a plan for what happens when the server fails, or data is deleted.

☐ Back up three copies of data

☐ Back up data in two file formats

☐ Have at least one backup in a separate location (Check out Chapter Five for more on the 3-2-1 Rule)

3

THE BEST LINE OF DEFENCE

IN THE LAST CHAPTER, I mentioned that your people are one of your strongest defences against cybercriminals. That's because education, common sense, and a reasonable level of alertness can make or break a cybersecurity strategy.

If your employees aren't aware of current threats or how to safely navigate emails and the web, or they don't know about connecting to unprotected Wi-Fi networks or how to use firewalls, then they unfortunately present a risk to your business and your data safety.

The problem that we see too often is that staff education gets ignored, with the brunt of IT strategy and defence falling back onto off-the-shelf software. We also see a widely spread belief (or hope) that cyberattacks are the sorts of things that happen to other people and other businesses – which, as we've seen, isn't remotely true.

The reality is that, even if you've mastered spam filtering, your firewalls are watertight, you've enabled some basic web filtering packages, you've got a decent antivirus, and you're keeping your systems up to date, a poorly-justified click or short-sighted download can be like giving cybercriminals the key to your back door.

There's a prevailing idea that it's the older staff who will make well-meaning mistakes like falling for scam and spam content, but in reality younger staffers – who have grown up with the internet as part of their daily lives – are at the same risk of making simple mistakes. No one's too clever or too practiced to fall for a scam, and those who think they're too clever to see a scam coming are the same ones who fall for sophisticated tricks.

Education is as much about unlearning bad habits as it is picking up good ones, which is why it's sometimes an uphill battle. But we can't solve problems with the same actions that got us into the situation, so re-thinking safety and strategy has to be a continuous activity, especially as new and more innovative scams and spam, and more complex systems and software are launched onto the market every year.

It's not just protecting your business against spam or viruses. You've got to protect your sensitive data from the inside as well, which is why best practices will help prevent internal fraud, keep your data safe when working with contractors, and improve your business's overall efficiency.

THE BASICS

When it comes to training your team, the first thing to teach are some of the classic tricks and traps of the game. We've talked about these briefly in earlier chapters. But there's always room to improve on human error, so let's look at some of the things to look out for.

SUSPICIOUS EMAILS

As we talked about in the last couple of chapters, most email platforms have a spam filter built in that stops some or most scam emails making their way to your inbox, or at least will quarantine them in a dedicated folder. Some emails just look suspicious, but if you're naïve or simply mistaken, then it's easy to click on an email – say, one that appears to be from a desperate family member stuck abroad – and have your data exploited.

Here are some things to check when you receive an email. For starters, ask yourself:

- Do I recognise the sender's email address?
- Is this email related to my usual job activities?
- Is this email impersonal, using 'customer' or 'to whom it may concern' rather than my name?
- Do I have a business relationship with this sender?
- Is there an unexpected attachment or hyperlink? Do the attachments make sense?
- Is the way in which this business is communicating typical of them?
- Am I expecting this invoice or bill from this client or business?
- Was I CC'd into this email with others that I recognise, or was it an odd or random mixture of people?
- When I hover over hyperlinks, does the link displayed match the description?
- Was this email sent inside normal business hours?
- Does the tone of voice match what I know of the sender? Is the spelling and grammar particularly out of the ordinary?
- What is the sender asking of me?
- Is the email asking me to view something compromising or embarrassing?
- Does the sender claim to have something for me that requires me to send money or personal information?

When it comes to training your staff on matters of email security, it can be helpful to ask them to go through these questions when they receive an email, and have them answer them as if they were justifying it to a colleague. If too many 'buts' get thrown up, then they might need some more education as to why it's dangerous to click risky links or download unsolicited attachments.

If you're suspicious about a link from someone you know, then remember you can still phone them or knock on their door and ask them personally about it. You might just be the first person to let them know if their security's been compromised.

Like all cybersecurity, the path towards inoculating your staff against scams is not a one-and-done event. Your staff will intellectually 'get' a one-pager security tip memo or email, or even sit through an hour-long seminar. But the moment they leave the room or dismiss the email, the data's dumped like a teenager writing off their calculus knowledge the second they leave their final maths exam.

For this reason, cybersecurity can't be considered a tick box on an annual check list, but instead needs to be incorporated into how you operate: through engaging systems and processes that ensure that all aspects of the organisation remain safe on an ongoing basis.

Liaise with your IT services provider and look to incorporate a training program that enables the entire team to receive ongoing exposure to the many ways a business can be subverted – and so increase their situational awareness.

PUBLIC WI-FI

A major issue facing your business is your employees connecting to unsecured Wi-Fi spots. It's an easy mistake to make, especially when every café or fast food joint offers internet for free nowadays.

The problem is that you never really know who's watching the data on a private network, or if the network you're looking at is the one you intended to connect to. Your local café might only have one network – 'Café Wi-Fi' – but the 'Café Wi-Fi: Staff' next on the list looks legitimate and doesn't require purchase for password. And when you connect to the fake 'Staff' network, someone in the carpark is stealing your banking data, reading your private Facebook messages, and setting up some ransomware on your disc.

As a general rule, it's better to prevent your staff from logging onto public networks – either through a policy or through settings on their devices. If you know that they need internet access while they're out and about, you're far better to ensure they've got some form of mobile data that is being used only by them.

DEVICE SECURITY

You and your team probably have work emails coming through on your work computer, a laptop, a tablet, and your mobile. Each of those is vulnerable to hacking (especially if you lose one!) so each needs at least one layer of password protection to keep it safe – something we talked about in the last chapter.

So what do you do if you realise you've lost one of your devices? The first thing is to block or wipe the device remotely, something which Apple and Samsung offer on most of their devices now, or that your managed IT services company should be able to do for you. This prevents a thief (or just someone who's found your device) from accessing the information on the device and potentially gaining access to the many other accounts that you are likely logged into. You'll also want to change all those account passwords (which you should be doing every 90 days regardless) just in case someone tries to read your emails or check your accounts.

MOBILE DEVICE MANAGEMENT & SECURITY

If you see suspicious activity while using your device, the steps you should take are a little different. Simple steps like disconnecting the machine from the network or powering it off can stop some damage in its tracks, but this should also be followed by notifying management of what's happened and organising a workaround. Any managed IT services provider worth their salt will be able to jump into action here and find out what's happened – and hopefully prevent any further damage as well. But prevention is always better than the cure.

As more and more business is conducted on mobile devices with software-as-a-service (SaaS) applications delivered by apps or via a web browser (think Google Drive, Dropbox or OneDrive, but also Cisco, Xero and the like), there will be a growing risk that confidential or commercially sensitive data will accumulate on smart phones and tablets. Android and Apple devices are not magically immune to cyber-attack, so to address this risk, endpoint security needs to extend towards these portable computing devices.

Organisations looking at this problem will be keenly aware that their data privacy is a primary concern. The best solution is a mobile device management platform that provides centralised control as well as mobile endpoint security and can go a step further into 'containerisation'. This is basically carving out a section of the phone's resources and storing all the company applications and any related data in an encrypted, walled-off section of the phone. Containerisation is very handy if the company policy encourages or allows team members to Bring Your Own Device (BYOD). If that device is lost or the person leaves, then the bits the company cares about are encrypted, and, if the company pushes a remote wipe command, then only the contents of that container will be purged and your people's personal holiday snaps won't be affected.

Ultimately, device security is as varied and complex as the devices themselves, which is why it's a smart move to work with a security specialist and IT management to ensure that both the devices themselves and the habits of your team are as watertight as possible.

WHO ARE YOUR ORGANISATION'S MOST VULNERABLE?

This is a question that I've often been asked, or had to ask myself when working with clients on their business's cybersecurity. Given the broad spread of attacks, human errors, and varying skills across a team – who's the most vulnerable?

The short answer? Everyone. As we've mentioned throughout this book, no one is immune to attack, and no one can be discounted from vulnerabilities. That's why you need so many layers of security working together so that your entire strategy helps mitigate and block attacks.

However, I know that's probably not the most useful answer when you're looking for somewhere to start!

The more productive answer is that it's usually your HR people, your CEOs, and your accounts people – or anyone who shares the most files – who are at the highest risk of exploitation.

HR

As we've seen, innocuous-looking files are great vehicles for attacks. Your HR people get CVs sent to them all day, every day (especially if you're a recruiting company). That means countless attachments, PDFs, links to OneDrive and Dropbox, and all sorts of file-sharing applications or sites. The problem is that these files could be literally anything – so your HR people, who are maybe handling more files than your average user, will possibly need a bit more training than your average staff member.

CEOS AND ACCOUNTS

CEOs and accounts people are excellent targets for cybercriminals, since they make the money flow in and out of an organisation. From an access perspective, they're the key to the front door, often with more access within their organisation's IT systems than they really need. Once someone has made it through the front door (so to speak) by infiltrating a CEO's emails, files, or logins, this access can then be leveraged to gain entry to even more.

Your accounts staff make fantastic targets since they're constantly receiving PDF invoices which are too easy to doctor up and create a legitimate attack. If you've ever looked at a spam folder, you'll see just how many of them have 'invoice' in the title. Instead, consider using a specific invoicing system or convention with your suppliers, to ensure that anything which doesn't follow those rules is immediately flagged as possible spam.

When it comes to making yourself more secure, take a moment to check out the access and liabilities of those who are accessing the most files, and the most vulnerable files, and be sure that they've got the protection and education they need.

WHO GETS ACCESS TO WHAT?

So you've identified that your top brass, the accounts people, and large file-sharers are the ones to train up to a different level and maybe add some extra protections. But as a growing business, there are plenty of other people involved – so how do you know who needs access to which parts of your IT systems?

That comes down to considering what people actually need to do their job well – and how to reduce your risk. If you're building an app, or simply scaling up, you may need a lot of people – and often quickly. Contractors will bring in their own devices, like laptops, which is a bonus in terms of keeping costs low. But this can also be a risk. If you're going to share critical data with those who aren't using devices owned by your company, then you need to ensure there's some top-level security architecture in place that protects the company's private information and intellectual property.

Beyond contractors though, there are considerations to make

around the people who have significant responsibility or owner-ship over areas of your business.

For example, people who often need extra attention are your office managers, or the people who are in sole charge of your finances. I have someone at Vertech who takes care of all our finances because, frankly, I'm not very good at them. I leave the specialist knowledge to those who know best – and who I trust.

However, that trust can make or break your business's secu-rity, and your finances. If you need someone to do an audit of your books on an annual basis, or keep tabs on every penny that's going out of your organisation, then you need to trust their work.

This is where savvy distribution of access comes in. Providing people access only to what they need, such as just invoicing instead of your entire financials, can be a good way to spread the risk and ensure you're not putting too much power in the hands of one person. Strategic, distributed access is incred-ibly important to make sure you're protecting your data, your business, and your customers.

You might think that the people you've hired are top notch, and could never do wrong, but even the most trustworthy people can fall for a clever scam. No one's too smart to be scammed or exploited. What's more, there are very credible people out there who are excellent at manipulation and scam-ming. Which brings us to ...

INTERNAL FRAUD

Cybercriminals and scammers aren't necessarily out to hurt you specifically – they're just opportunists who are out for them-selves. That doesn't excuse their actions, but it's important to remember that you need to look at your access and cybersecurity critically and objectively.

But attacks come from the inside as well. While we want to believe we've hired the right people, trained them well and they'll serve us and our organisations well for years to come, sadly, that's not always the case – particularly with SMEs.

Internal fraud is a serious issue, particularly because it takes advantage of our trusting nature as Kiwis. As an SME, you're exponentially more likely to be a victim of internal fraud – and with an average rip-off level of $200,000 – than if you're a major corporation. Exactly why isn't clear, but it could be down to what scammers think they can get away with, especially with smaller operations where there aren't necessarily the most robust systems in place.

What we've seen is that the average length over which an internal fraud crime occurs is about 36 months – and the fraud-sters use that time to build trust, erode security, and exploit a little at a time. But it's not a totally random act. Fraudsters need three things:

Motive

More often than not, fraud is about money. A fraudster wants more than they're getting currently, so will use what power and opportunities they have available to their advantage. Fraud might also be to favour a particular client, or to fudge numbers so that their performance looks better. Maybe they're claiming for more time than they've actually used, or for 'business expenses' that are actually them and their spouse enjoying a Friday night together.

Rationalisation

This is where they'll argue to themselves that what they're doing is justified. Ethics goes out of the window as a fraudster uses all the tools in their arsenal to explain away the abuse – often with particular emphasis on 'Well, it's not a problem if I don't get caught.' That the company won't miss a few dollars here and there, or that they've got enough as it is so why shouldn't the fraudster take what's 'owed' them? It might equally be about sending a message – if there's a gap, why not exploit it? Which leads us to …

Opportunity

This is the only one that you, as a business owner, have control over. Restrict opportunities and prevent them from tempting people. Plug the holes in that bucket before the water gets in. Put in processes that simply make it much more difficult for someone to even contemplate it. That can start with the HR process – making sure you're implementing thorough police and/or background checks, or speaking to previous managers and business owners they've been working for.

Again, trust is a big thing here. Let's say you're a small company and your partner or a close family member has been handling accounts and payroll for years. At some point, you need to hand that position on to someone else – an external person who is yet to earn that trust, but has it thrust upon them. This is especially common if you're experiencing rapid growth and need to scale operations quickly – you can often settle for 'good enough' because you need bums on seats.

The trick is to remove the subjectivity. Work with IT systems that are auditable and that can provide you traceable and evidential freezes on accounts. We do a lot of this at Vertech, because our clients know that there's a need for robust account-ability at all levels and that an attitude of 'good enough' is what catches some companies out.

Here are some other techniques and approaches that will help maintain your internal security:

— Separate the person who enters the bills from the person who pays the bills – a simple step, but one that's often over-looked or ignored for the sake of convenience. Go a step further and make it such that the person who enters the bills can't enter the Payee Bank Account number.

— Rotate roles on a regular basis so that no one person can work a scam for any length of time without the possibility that the next person might spot it. It also has the side benefit of ensuring there is redundancy of capabilities within the accounts team!

— Set up mandatory periods of leave so that accounts people

have to hand over their duties to another person. A good accounts person should document how they handle the critical tasks in the business so that another person can step in if they are sick. If they go on holiday but still insist on remoting in to do the bills or payroll, then this is a red flag.

— Bills should only be paid on one (or maybe two) set days of the month, such that you have time to scrutinise the changes and easily compare them to a previous payment run.

— 29% of all fraud detection comes because of a tip-off, so another thing you can do is to set up an evidential hotline for ethical reporting in your business. If someone spots something suspect or someone doing something wrong – ripping off a customer, fudging numbers or doing something that doesn't feel right – then you have a lifeline in place. Sometimes you just need to step back and get some external, objective perspective.

The other thing to look out for are the warning signs of internal fraud. Some red flags could include individuals with financial troubles of their own, living beyond their means, a history of excessive debts, lifestyle changes, gambling, marital problems, an unusually close relationship with a customer/vendor, or that they never take any leave or give up control to anyone. It could be a spike in the number of invoices from a particular supplier or group of suppliers, along with a muddling of documentation and records.

If you're in those kinds of situations, or you're aware of those kinds of things, then just reach out to your accountant or someone external. Ask them to take a deep look into your books and make sure they're watertight. Then get professional advice on what kind of systems you can put in place to preserve their propriety. This is simply making sure that everything appears above board and that no one can be accused of the slightest possibility that they have abused their position of trust.

Local Admin Access & the Least Privilege Principle

As a business owner, you can't be in control of everyone's systems at all times and maintain both a good working relationship and your productivity. So, once you start scaling beyond, say, five people in your team, you need to start putting in place some clear policies as to who can do what and when. This is often achieved with local administrator passwords.

Just as web filtering limits who can access which websites and when, restricting administrator rights to a machine is a key part of a cybersecurity strategy. Restricting admin access means that you're not letting just anybody and everybody install whatever they want on their machine at any time.

Realistically, most people within an organisation are doing a set role, a set job, and within set applications, so there's little practical demand for extra applications. There are big risks associated with downloading stuff from the internet or trying out free (or 'freemium') applications – especially from an intellectual property perspective – so it never hurts to restrict the ability to do that. If you have sensitive client data – say you're a marketing firm or a health care company – and you upload that onto a free service, then you've effectively handed that confidential and private data to a third party provider.

Read the service level agreements (SLAs) of any programme, because you might be agreeing that anything you put in their systems they can then use and re-sell. Remember, nothing's ever really 'free' – if it looks that way, it's because you're the product.

* * *

SLA
The 'service-level agreement', the terms that define what a customer can expect from a supplier, how the supplier can use customer data, and more. Remember those terms and conditions you never read? Those are your SLAs.

* * *

Going further up the chain, you need to consider stricter restrictions for all. As much as your staff may want to try out new things, the ground underneath you can shift very quickly. When your company is small, your staff will wear a bunch of different hats; as you grow in operational maturity, then staff roles will become more specialised. A shift in mindset is needed from a relaxed and permissive work culture (i.e. who cares, since you need the work done now) to one where you grant access only to what people need for their roles.

Data access can become linked to a job role, which makes it easy for a manager to assign rights, and for the IT admins to support the environment. If you leave it as a free-for-all then you are taking great risks with one of your biggest assets.

So how does this link us to cybersecurity? Well, it circles us back around to web filtering and application control again. It doesn't mean that you can't ever let your team install programs on their computers, but that there needs to be some oversight and justification as to what they're downloading and why. Think about what's necessary to do the job at hand, and if it's not going to be helping with productivity, then you probably don't need it.

Checklist

Suspicious emails and messages.

I included a pretty comprehensive list at the beginning of the chapter, so here's a shorter version:

☐ Do I recognise the sender's email address?

☐ Is this email impersonal, referring to me as 'customer' rather than my name?

☐ Am I expecting attachments or links from this person, and do the attachments or hyperlinks make sense? Does the hyperlink match the description?

☐ Is this a normal method of communication for the sender?

☐ Does the language sound like the sender?

☐ Is the sender asking something out of the ordinary from me?

☐ Is the email asking me to view something compromising, embarrassing or otherwise not safe for work?

☐ Is the sender asking me to send money, credit card details

☐ Can I call the sender to clarify the details of their email?

Public Wi-Fi

☐ Engage a web/device filter to block public Wi-Fi use on your team's work devices

☐ Never connect to an unsecured Wi-Fi network

☐ Use a Private VPN to ensure your traffic is encrypted end to end

☐ Better yet, use your own mobile hotspot

Team training & Access

☐ Set up a remote device management system to track/block/wipe devices remotely if lost

☐ Change your passwords every 90 days

☐ Establish 'containerisation' on devices to wall off sensitive information and services

Device Management & Security

☐ Undertake regular cybersecurity training sessions

☐ Focus attention on HR, CEOs, accounts people and those who send and receive files the most

☐ Create access permission layers for your staff so that they have only the tools they need

☐ Set limits to what can be downloaded (remember – nothing's ever really 'free')

Internal security

☐ Separate the person who enters the bills from the person who pays them

☐ Rotate roles regularly to ensure no one person can work a scam for too long

☐ Focus bill payments onto one day a month

☐ Establish a secure evidence hotline so your staff can safely provide tip-offs

☐ Have external people assess your accounts regularly to ensure they're watertight

A closer look: DSL Logistics' cybersecurity strategy

DSL Logistics provide third-party contract warehousing and distribution, international freight forwarding and customs clearance services for clients, based out of their operations centre in Mangere, Auckland. After some early experiences with spam, DSL implemented a comprehensive cybersecurity system – including staff training – and the impact has been huge.

Recognising the reality of digital business

Philip Rashleigh of DSL Logistics has been in business a long time. Since he started using emails, he's seen the potential for issues coming through his inboxes and the hassles that viruses can cause.

"Back in the early days when emails got started," he says, "we got hit with a couple of viruses when staff clicked on attachments that they thought looked cool – as often happened back then.

"The early viruses were more annoying than anything. They'd do silly things when you started up your computer, or say undesirable words out loud."

But Philip soon realised the emails were a potential source of other issues for DSL. Like many businesses, most of their information is in databases – and they needed far better protection than anything else. If something were to happen to that data, they'd be up a certain creek.

"We had an issue about six years ago, when something sneaked through that looked quite legitimate – but it was ransomware that encrypted our files and asked for money."

Thankfully, they were lucky – as soon as they recognised the encryption was happening they stopped it, removed it, and had a good back-up in place.

Building strength in layers

Over the last 25-odd years, Philip's used services like Web Marshall and Mail Marshall to protect his computers. More recently, though, we've helped him build his arsenal and protect the business from spam and while browsing.

"We always had firewalls on our network – even back when we were on ADSL – to stop intrusion but still allow traffic through," he says.

Now he's layered up his security with antivirus, and putting good back-ups in place. He's set up systems that mean his emails get checked twice before they get to a person, and also archiving and backing up everything, just in case an attack does get through.

DSL have also implemented dark web scanning with DSL, searching the dark web and getting alerted if their email addresses and logins show up. They keep on top of firewall upgrades and make sure they're up to date with all our software.

People first

However, key to their success hasn't been technology – it's been people. Philip recognises better than most that the work at DSL is about people, and it's for them that they need to keep their security and systems optimal.

"We employ over a hundred staff, and if our systems were to go down, we wouldn't be able to provide work for them. We run about 18 hours on, 6 off, and we've all got families who rely on their family members to come to work and get paid. If we couldn't do that, they're impacted – as are our customers, who rely on us to get their products to store. So it makes a difference keeping things running."

Every one or two months, the staff at DSL will go through online training – getting reminders of the type of things to look out for and learning about possible new threats. In between, we'll run test campaigns to check who's been paying attention – sending out a 'malicious' email that looks legitimate. It won't do anything harmful, but it's great to see who's exercising best practices.

Today, the staff have become excellent at spotting these. "They won't open up something they're not sure about, or they'll come and ask." Their people are DSL's final line of defence. Even if something gets through all the other nets, the team have got an eye out for anything that looks suspect to make sure it doesn't stop them running. That relies not just on good maintenance – it's also about keeping the people up to speed.

If you were to look at DSL's firewalls and archives, you'd see that cybercriminals are attempting to break into their systems virtually constantly. Had even one of those broken through, the business could have been significantly impacted and may have had to stop trading.

By taking a strategic, all-encompassing approach to cybersecurity – with multiple lines of defence – DSL have been able to stop those from coming through. This proactive approach has been vital to keeping the business running – and keeping their customers happy.

4

YOU'RE GOING TO BE SCAMMED

EVERY YEAR, SCAMWATCH ISSUE THEIR SUMMARY of what's been happening in the cybersecurity space worldwide. The results are either surprising or unsurprising, depending on your view.

For instance, in 2019, CERT NZ reported that scams and fraud accounted for $14.5 million of loss, with a staggering 53 percent increase in scams and fraud reports from 2018.

The average loss is just shy of $6,000 per person that got scammed. Scams and fraud topped the list once again in terms of the amount of money lost because of them, respectively tapping into our wants for more cash, more romance (or near offer).

Scams have long worked – and continue to work – through a combination of the con artist's confidence and ability to gain trust, and in their ability to exploit the ignorance, naivety, credulity, vanity, greed, or compassion of the victim. What's changed is that the con artist has gone digital – along with the rest of the world.

The internet is still relatively young, as far as technology goes, and the rate of change is breakneck. That makes for a dangerous combination. It's too easy for the con artist to take advantage of the gap between a new technology or service coming out and the average person's understanding. Twenty years ago, phone-based scams were king; they're still pretty common (around 100,000 reported every year, costing around $30 million), but it's a shrinking market.

Now cons are online, hidden by the semi-private nature of the internet, promising investment opportunities or romance, or exploiting our passwords, invoices, email lists and devices. That's how they walk away with a hundred million dollars every year – often taken at anything from ten dollars to a few thousand at a time.

While the technology has changed, the cons themselves are just variations of older practices. For example:

— Pretexting is when someone pretends to be a high-up member of your organisation, but via email rather than a phone call or letter.

— Quid Pro Quo is a tempting invite for cheap or free digital services, rather than the physical goods that Baiting offered in the back pages of certain newspapers.

— Tailgating is when an unauthorised person physically follows one of your team into a restricted area. This hasn't really changed, it's just that cybercriminals might be there to get network access via an email, rather than wandering into an office.

Here's what else hasn't changed: most people don't know that they've been conned until it's too late. It takes an average of 191 days for a company to realise it's been compromised by a data breach, if they realise at all. Are you prepared to lose half a year's worth of data?

Just like the fact that someone out there is looking for weaknesses in your cybersecurity, someone out there is opportunistically trying to pull the wool over your eyes right now. But as always, the trick is to take a proactive approach to cybersecurity to ensure that you're protected from all sides: that you've got layered network protections, you're not giving every staff member wholesale access to your systems if that's not needed, and that your team know what to look for so that they realise what a scam looks like – before it's too late.

PASSWORD SCAMS

We've talked throughout this book about passwords – why you need a good password manager rather than a little black book or Excel spreadsheet; why they should be private things; and how easily they give criminals access to your data.

Even if you've done well and kept your passwords secure, it's still possible to fall for password scams.

There are a few variations of the password scam, and like most scams, they are great at taking advantage of our suscepti-bility to click on links that look legitimate – but in reality, aren't. Let's take a look at the scraping kind of scam that often comes through your inbox or via a legitimate-looking website and tricks you into putting in your details.

Businesses now send most of their bills and invoices via email or using document-sharing tools like DocuSign. With a scam, you'll be invited to click through to review the documents, and that link will take you off to a corrupted website, and invite you to make an account or put in your login details.

What complicates this type of document-approval password scam is that these types of emails often get through your filters because they're coming from a legitimate email account, not a dodgy one. For all intents and purposes, your antivirus protec-tion hasn't seen anything wrong. The website link isn't neces-sarily on any blacklist for serving up malicious code, so your malware might not have put up red flags for you (and often won't until someone manually raises the issue).

The first giveaway that this sort of thing is risky is that if you hover over the 'click here' links, you'll see they can have suspect URLs – something we've talked about previously. As always, my recommendation is to hover over the link and make a decision.

Look at whether it matches what the email sender is talking to you about or not.

If you do click through, you might get served up a page that looks like the real Dropbox, or DocuSign, or the bank you have your business accounts with. So you put in your email details and your password, thinking that you're about to download some documents or get paid, and hackers now have a key password (and, as we talked about in Chapter Two, probably the password you use for everything!).

It's easy to fall for these kinds of scams because they often look and feel real enough. But we always have to turn back to the first principles: if in doubt, pause and check. And don't click the link if it's from somebody you don't know, or if it's come through with links to websites or resources that the sender's never used before. The other quick solution is to give the sender a quick phone call and check in. It might take a minute longer, but you may save yourself a world of pain – and tip them off to the fact their email's been compromised.

BUSINESS EMAIL COMPROMISE & INVOICE SCAMS

There a couple of different types of invoice scams out there, and like password scams, they tend to get through the door by dressing the part.

The first type of invoice scam involves the scammer sending through a legitimate-looking invoice for, say, a printer company that they know has recently done work for you. All the scammer has done is given you a hard-to-trace bank account that you happily put your payment into, and suddenly they're a few dollars up. The alternative version of this scam works especially well in larger companies where the staff who arrange payments aren't always in good communication with the wider team: an invoice will come through from an authentic-sounding business – usually for services, rather than goods – and your staff will pay it without thinking. Again, a phone call can clear this sort of thing up.

As recently as 2019, an NZ kids' charity fell victim to this to the tune of $45,000 of grant money, after the account director received emails supposedly from the charity's director asking for two offshore payments via online banking. Pretty disgusting stuff on the cybercriminal's part.

The other type of invoice scam is a variation on the email scam that piggybacks off a business's payments – especially around the 20th of the month, when bills are usually issued. As above, sometimes the mismatch between link title and URL will give away that something's up. Sometimes you'll notice that the company on the invoice, or the software (think QuickBooks, Intuit or Xero) doesn't correspond with any of your clients' services. Again, the links might not be blacklisted or flagged as dodgy because they're too new, so a well-meaning or naïve click can open the door for malware to come through.

If you've ignored all the red flags and clicked the mis-matched link, you might be taken to a download page. The download looks like a pdf, but has its true extension hidden, meaning once you've clicked it a .zip folder might start making its way into your system.

Again, though, you might have made it this far (though you really shouldn't have!), and you might then scan the .zip folder for viruses. A big giveaway that malware is waiting for you is if you see files with an .exe or .vbs extension (as opposed to .pdf or .docx). Many people have file suffixes turned off for aesthetics, but it's just making it easier for people to get tricked and let the malware run wild on your networks and your data.

If you do see suspect links and files making their way in, then stop, purge the files, and train your anti-spam program to take it out of the link and verify it.

SEXTORTION SCAMS, AKA THE WEBCAM SCAM ON STEROIDS

I'm often called out to help clients who are a bit freaked out. An email will have popped up in their inbox, and while it doesn't have any malware attached, it does have a very specific threat in the email body.

The messages vary, but they're generally along the lines of "I know you've been visiting XYZ site and what you've been doing in front of your webcam. If you don't want the video sent to all your contacts, then pay us bitcoin…"

It's a variation of the sextortion scam I mentioned in Chapter Two, but here's the difference: the scammers will incite real fear and 'prove' how legitimate they are by sending you an old password that you've used. This is basically the threat of blackmail, and it's a powerful threat because it sets us up for public embarrassment in a big way. Plus, they've got your password – so what else do they have?

This was a serious problem for thousands of people, in 2018 in the US, who shelled out almost half a million dollars to hold sextortionists at bay.

The reality is that these scams are full of hot air. Generally, when I take a look at a client's computer and run multiple scans, I'll find no malware or rootkits. There is probably no webcam video. But what about the password?

This happens when you use the same password for multiple accounts, and for a long time. When I look up the user's email address on HaveIBeenPwned.com, I'll see that their details have been leaked as part of a LinkedIn, Dropbox, or any other mass hacking of data. It's yesterday's breadcrumbs. It's a great idea from the scammer's perspective to incorporate that password because it makes the threat seem so much more real – and more likely for someone to fall for it out of fear of public embarrassment.

That being said, it is possible – but avoidable – for hackers to access any network-linked camera, be that a webcam, an unprotected security camera or even a nanny camera. So, once you've layered up with your antiviral and anti-malware software, kept on top of dodgy links, shored up your firewall and all the other aspects, buy yourself a sliding webcam cover to physically block the camera when it's not in use.

There's a lot of fun to be had on the internet, but keep yourself safe.

EMAIL SCAMS

More recently I've been seeing the email combo attack. It's a variation of what we've seen before, usually: the promise of files to download, a link to Dropbox and an invite to input your details. The part that catches people out is that the link to download might have come from a reliable source, who in turn has had their email account hacked and the cybercriminal at the other end is using it to spread malware or widen the circle of exploitation.

Once you've clicked through and input your details, though, from there it can go three ways.

The first is the sextortion-type video claims, like the above webcam scam demanding untraceable currency in exchange for a video of you in a private moment.

The second type, often bundled with the first, is to download your address list and send out another round of scam or malware emails to your contacts, taking advantage of your contacts' trust that you're sending them something safe.

The last type is far scarier than the others. The cybercriminal uses your login details to set up an email forwarder – not on your computer itself, but linked to your Google or Microsoft account. And then they watch, and wait for trigger words like 'invoice' or 'bank account' so they can jump into the conversation as 'you' and reply to the sender with updated bank account details. When this happens to our clients, the first thing we do is look for the forwarder (and bin it!), then search their network history for any malware that might be waiting in the wings.

From a scammer's point of view, the mass email chain is pretty effective – sooner or later they'll get enough people to make it worth their while, and in the meantime they can make some quick money with a sextortion or other scam.

A variation of this happened to multimedia giant British Pathé, British fashion retailer Matalan, and the US publisher Pantheon Books. Their Twitter accounts were hacked to promise Bitcoin-related benefits to their followers and the scammers walked off with over £120,000 (around $230,000 NZD).

The solution? As always, it's about changing your passwords on a regular basis, monitoring on your domain name, and getting your IT provider to stop users from being able to forward their own emails. This last solution can be a bit of a pain, but every block makes it harder for these sorts of scams to take hold.

VOICE SCAMS AND ROBOCALLS

> Hey. Since you've come so much from several countries, we will be changing your IP address within the router free of charge. Please press one to connect with the technician, press two to disconnect the line.

The above is a real voice message, verbatim, that one of my clients received. And it has the hallmarks of a voice scam: the bad English, the jargon, the slightly confusing premise that invites follow-up.

Voice scams have been around as long as automatic phone diallers have existed. They work much like the mass email linking we've explored: sooner or later they'll hit on someone vulnerable or naïve and wipe them out.

Again, there are a few ways you can be taken advantage of via the phone.

The most common are 'phishing' calls from hidden or fake caller IDs that promise easy money. They may pretend to be from your internet or phone provider or a big company like Microsoft or Apple, 'helpfully' telling you how to remove malware they've 'detected' on your computer or phone – while simply opening the door to let themselves into your computer. They equally could be forceful and threatening, perhaps telling you that one small payment will stop the debt collectors knocking on the door, or that your credit card has been compromised and you just need to 'confirm' your details with them before they can help you further.

Often these calls will come from blocked, private, or international numbers, or there is a significant delay in their responses as the call bounces to a call centre on the other side of the world. But it is possible to spoof a telephone number, just as it's possible to spoof an email address, and appear to be coming from an authentic source.

Healthy scepticism goes a long way here. It's hardly likely that the customer service branches of these big companies have teams dedicated to calling their clients to inform them of breaches. It just doesn't make sense. It's also worth remembering that, via the phone, companies don't ask for your passwords, request your credit details or money, threaten to disconnect your internet, or ask for access to your computer. So, if this happens, the best thing to do is simply hang up and block the number. Don't pursue it.

If there is a legitimate issue, then they'll get back to you – and often through the post, or to invite you into a store to sort it securely and in person.

As I mentioned earlier in this book, the gap between a new technology and the public's understanding is a gap cybercriminals like to extort. The example I used at the start of this section is slightly more believable than the phone examples, since it sounds inviting, and to the uninitiated, the offer to change your IP address in your router for free might be a good thing, right?

Well, as the old saying goes, if it sounds too good to be true then it probably is. There's no such thing as a free lunch. Upgrades to your IT are best left to your IT manager or paid professionals.

It's worth noting that robocall scams and the like are getting more sophisticated. Some are variations of existing 'honey pot' traps but via the fast-moving world of dating apps like Tinder, inviting users to click through for more provocative content. We've seen cybercriminals exploit family group chats in messaging apps like WhatsApp, pretending to be a family member in an urgent and vulnerable position and in need of a short-term loan. The rest plays out as expected.

The foundations for the next generation of scams are already being laid. Take, for example, the increasingly powerful machine-learning 'deep fakes' that can mimic the voices (and faces) of celebrities by listening to (and watching) recordings. With enough data – i.e., if they've been quietly listening in to your phone calls or conversations long enough via malware on your devices – then it's possible that they could effectively mimic your voice or the voice of a colleague, friend or family member on the phone (but perhaps not your mannerisms – at least not yet).

Let's complicate things further. In 2018, Google demoed an enhanced voice assistant service that could, apparently, book an appointment for a haircut via the phone by speaking to a real person. What was remarkable were the natural-sounding hesitations and pauses that the AI generated, making the voice seem, well, human. Soon we may not know whether we're speaking to a real person on the other end or not. And when that time comes, we'll have to develop some new measures to protect us.

GOOGLE MAPS SCAMS

Chances are you use Google Maps regularly, since, alongside Apple, they have the lion's share of the online and mobile app market.

When you Google something, you'll generally be directed to the Google Maps page and company listing with its website and phone number there for the clicking. It's not necessarily the most reliable way for you to get your information.

A lot of what's show in Google Maps is publicly listed, and the business owner, or indeed anyone else like a Google Local Guide, can come in and edit things like trading hours, website addresses and phone numbers.

Sometimes the Local Guides' information is helpful, or far from malicious. There's a great example of this in Hobson Bay near Parnell in Auckland, where users are able to mark trails on Maps, and someone drew a cute picture of a cat. It's harmless and a bit of fun.

Contrast that with the more sinister case recently in India, where con artists are using their Guide accounts to create fake entries representing a local bank, putting their own telephone number in. People look up the bank's details and see their closest branch, give the con artists a call, and innocently give over their card information, their pins, the CCV on their Visas. Remember: if you're talking to a real bank, they're not going to ask for that information.

The lesson to take away is that you shouldn't start the call from a Google search or the Google Maps page; go through to the actual website and look for their details on a contact page. There you've got a much better chance of finding the correct info, and to avoid being scammed.

SIM SWAP ATTACKS

In 2019, Twitter CEO Jack Dorsey's own Twitter account claimed that the company's San Francisco HQ would soon be bombed, followed by a string of anti-Semitic slurs and racist posts. Dorsey had been possibly the highest profile user on the platform to have fallen victim to the so-called SIM swap attack.

Since 3G came about in 2003 (and launched in NZ in 2008), most cell phones have used subscriber identity module (SIM) cards to connect to their respective networks. Previously your phone number was coded to your phone through the network, but now it could be moved from device to device through the small SIM card chip.

The SIM swap attack takes advantage of just this, usually by combining social engineering with some low-level questions and a weakness of the one-time passwords sent via text. The scam artist will often start by gathering some personal details about the user – phishing for or researching from online presences those easily answerable questions about first schools, mums' maiden names, first pets. If you've left that kind of information out there – like on Instagram posts or tweets – then you're making it easy for scammers to take advantage of you. They can also phish you and put the pressure on: say you're a single mum, the baby's crying in the background, and they can ask 'just one more quick question' to sort out their query – and make it easy for them.

The scammer will then convince the phone company to switch the victim's phone number to a fraudulent SIM – often by impersonating the victim and using the information they've collated to answer personal questions. Once the victim's phone number is in the hands of the scam artist, they can then receive one-time passwords (e.g. via text) and gain access to bank accounts, social network data, iCloud backups, or anything that relies on text or phone calls to verify. Besides the risks of data loss, there's also the risk of exploitation of your personal information – bringing us back around to the webcam scam (with the potential threat made real if you have compromising photos in your iCloud stream, as famously occurred in 2015 with the celebrity photo hack).

Firstly, take care of what you post and leave out there, and be especially mindful of the security questions for your bank, your social accounts, and anywhere that you've got that sort of personal info linked to your data.

INVESTMENT SCAMS

Investment scams have been in the lead for the most money conned out of people for a few years running, accounting for around $40 million per year, most of which is claimed from men over 45. They usually take the same shape: a promise of 'low-risk, high-reward, fast turnaround' investments based on stock tips, initial public offerings, trading platforms, or Bitcoin-type offers. And sure, who wouldn't want to make a quick buck with minimal effort (after all, gambling is a billion-dollar industry). Just because there's a glossy brochure and smooth-talking salesman backed by a flash website, doesn't mean it's legitimate.

Remember, if it sounds too good to be true, it probably is.

ROMANCE SCAMS

There's good reason that romance scams are #2 on the most common scams lists, accounting for around $25 million dollars every year: people crave connections.

Romance scams are often long-term exploitations, starting with instant messaging through dating sites or social media. An apparently genuine relationship seems to build over time. You share a ton of emails, texts, telephones, and potentially photos; they tap into certain emotional triggers, playing delicate games of give-and-take, faking arguments so that it doesn't seem too good. They start soliciting gifts – perhaps objects delivered to their address, or even plane tickets to meet you.

But of course, it's a con. They can clean out people's bank accounts and leave significant financial and emotional damage to the sufferers.

Anyone can fall victim to a romance scam. While it may seem that often men are often more likely to be selected (though less likely to report it – especially if it complicates existing relationships), the data shows that women over 40 are more likely to fall victim to a romance scam.

The lesson here is not to believe anything unless – or until – you see it with your own eyes. Especially when it comes with the promise of romance.

SCAMS CHECKLIST

Importantly, like all checklists in this book, this is just a starting point. Our recommendation is that you engage with a professional IT firm to ensure that your cybersecurity meets your business's needs.

Password
- ☐ Destroy the 'little black book' of passwords
- ☐ Check for and block dodgy links
- ☐ Use good judgement when following links
- ☐ Get a secure password management tool
- ☐ Change your passwords regularly
- ☐ Use passphrases like greencyclingrabbit

Invoice
- ☐ Confirm bank details separately, especially if they've recently changed
- ☐ Check the invoice is legitimate by verifying via known telephone/txt/fax
- ☐ If in doubt, don't download
- ☐ Scan downloads
- ☐ Don't open .exe files

Extortion and sextortion

☐ Change your passwords regularly

☐ Cover your webcam (ask me for a free cover)

Email

☐ Ensure your antivirus security is up-to-date (as per Chapter Two)

☐ Scan your mailboxes for automatic forwarding

Voice scams and robocalls

☐ Use cautious care when receiving calls from authoritative-sounding sources

☐ Never give away passwords or critical info to a caller

☐ Keep your personal information close to your chest

Google Maps

☐ Go to the company's website for their contact details rather than via the Maps link

SIM swaps

☐ Keep your private information – like maiden names – off the internet

☐ Request extra security with your service and phone providers

☐ Change passwords regularly!

Investment

☐ Always seek a second opinion from someone qualified who you trust

☐ Remember large pay-outs always come with greater risks

Romance

☐ If it sounds too good to be true, it probably is

☐ It's always a small sum at first, a wedge to bigger favours

☐ Exercise best judgement

☐ Believe nothing!

A CLOSER LOOK: SCAMS AND CONS, BIG AND SMALL

It's often the case that you hear about the biggest scams – the ones where scammers walk off with millions of dollars from big companies. Take, for example, when Emirates Team NZ thought they were sending a seven-figure sum in response to a contractor's invoice, but that money ended up instead going into a Hungarian bank account. At time of writing, the Hungarian and NZ authorities are working together to get to the bottom of things, and Team NZ have denied any wrongdoing or fraud.

That sort of story makes front-page news. What often doesn't are the smaller scams, like those targeted at logistics companies.

Here's a recent one that's been getting some airtime in cyber-security circles. Logistics companies have received legitimate-looking paperwork claiming that some shipping containers require payment before they could leave their countries of origin and head to NZ.

Normally, the policy would be that a payment would have to come through from a client before the orders would go out, but the scammer knows this. (They may have been someone who works in the industry, like a customs or logistics worker themselves.) So they added an urgency to their communications, telling the victim that 'It has to be done now' or that they've received pressure from their (fictional) bosses and that you're somehow helping them out. Throw in some fake credit card details and a bit of photoshop document manipulation and it's easy enough to win over someone.

Of course, with a con like this, they don't have to succeed every time. As we've seen, as long as a scam works often enough, it's working. These invoices were for about $600. If a scammer sends out 100 of these, but only strikes lucky on one out of every ten, then that can still mean $6,000 in their bank account by the end of the day at no risk to themselves.

5

BUSINESS AS USUAL

WHAT PLAN DOES YOUR BUSINESS HAVE in place to recover from an IT disaster?

We all know how much we're relying on digital technology. And it's not just needing maps on your phone or streaming music instead of playing CDs like we used to in the 90s.

The more we come to rely on cloud-based computing and remote servers, the more opportunities there are for plain old human error, hardware failure, or cybersecurity attacks to take down businesses' abilities to function.

When things turned to custard in early 2020 with the COVID-19 pandemic, many businesses scrambled to stay the course. They shuttered their brick-and-mortar stores for the while and did their best to continue business as usual (or as near as possible) online. But that opened up huge opportunities for exploitation by cybercriminals and revealed the weaknesses in their existing IT infrastructures. As we mentioned in an earlier chapter, one report said that 43% of cyberattack victims in 2019 were small businesses. With the surge in online reliance in 2020, cyberattacks increased significantly, with estimates in the UK showing an increase in malicious email traffic from 12% before their lockdown started in March to over 60% six weeks later. We can expect similar numbers on a New Zealand level.

In fact, every time there's a global news story that pushes a narrative of fear, uncertainty and doubt (commonly called the 'FUD Factor'), cybercriminals leap to exploit people's desire for trustworthy resources. They take advantage of our tendency to bypass our normal cognitive defences in the face of FUD.

Cybercriminals' efforts extended to exploit the rising popularity of 'work from home'-related systems such as Zoom and Google Classroom so that their phishing campaigns would have a higher click rate. By February 2020, thousands of new domain names relating to COVID-19 were being registered per week for all sorts of purposes, and not all were to be trusted. According to security researchers, up to 20% (some 2,200 websites!) were considered suspicious.

So, even in an emergency, or in the middle of a news story like this, you cannot afford to lower your guard. From a cybercriminal's perspective, you are even more vulnerable – and easier to exploit. The chance of suffering further business interruption only goes up.

Business interruption is real – and so are the costs, both financial and your employees' and clients' lost trust. So, how do you protect yourself from downtime?

* * *

Business continuity planning
The ongoing process of creating, testing and re-evaluating your business's ability to continue operating in the face of potential threats. This can include information about what should happen to equipment, supplies and suppliers, locations, documents and documentation, and procedures.

* * *

DISASTER RECOVERY

We don't like to spend a lot of time thinking about worst-case scenarios like server failure or malware encryption of our files, which is exactly why we need to. Truth be told, planning for disasters is difficult, boring, earns you no money and you might never need it. Might is the key word here. If you do need it, that relatively small amount of planning and investment in disaster recovery can mean the difference between being able to dust yourself off after a painful event, or getting knocked out permanently – along with the closure of your business and a heavy impact upon everyone's livelihoods.

Disaster recovery encompasses the policies, procedures, and tools you have in place to handle an IT disaster so that you can keep your business running with minimum impact. It's playing the 'what-if' game with your IT set-up, anticipating what happens when a key piece of infrastructure goes down and what it'll take to get you back on the road.

Most of us have a vague idea what disaster recovery looks like, especially when we think about losing our phones or spilling water on a laptop. First, there's the pain of having to buy a new unit, but then there's the matter of having to load all our details back up. Nowadays, we rely on cloud storage automatically pulling in all our settings and apps, but if you're of a certain age you'll know the pain of having to manually type all your contacts' numbers into a new phone.

Your business's IT systems are a bit like that, except instead of being without your phone for a couple of hours, you're losing valuable client data, time, and money with every passing minute that your systems are down.

In Chapter One, we talked about security systems and how our clients' firewall logs looked like a window on a winter's day, with a constant stream of attacks raining down. Well, disaster recovery is both what happens when you discover that the bottom floor of your house is flooded, and the actions you need to take to dry out your home. Whilst we mainly deal with the IT side of things and enable an overall disaster recovery strategy, as a business owner you need to consider all of the risks – whether it's fire, flood, earthquake, theft, vandalism, pandemic, volcano or cybercrime!

From our perspective, if we can make your IT systems water-tight, then there's a very good chance that your disaster recovery plans will be flexible enough to deal with all but the most horrific scenarios.

So, what does it take to be prepared and what do you need to have in place as part of your disaster recovery plan?

TIME IS MONEY: THE RECOVERY TIME OBJECTIVE (RTO)

One of the first things you and your IT professionals should be asking is how much time you have between an incident and getting things back up and running. How soon can we have your systems operational after your server goes down, your system crashes, or you lose data?

We call this window the 'Recovery Time Objective' (RTO). If we're thinking about the rain getting into the house, then this is how long between the water getting in and doing damage, and getting the leaks patched and the carpet dried out so that you can carry on as usual – and ideally with minimal loss of data.

Just as you'll want to spot the water damage and get it sorted as soon as possible, in an ideal world the RTO will be as short a period as possible. For some companies, one or two days is acceptable; for others, an hour is too long.

In plain business terms, that's because your time is money. When a crash happens and your IT systems are offline, you lose money with every passing hour. If you've got 15 staff paid $25 per hour, then every hour is costing you $375. With a 9-hour workday, this downed workforce is costing you $3,375 every day!

Then there's the cost to get a skilled IT engineer to start

putting together your damaged network (assuming there is anything to recover and there are the hardware and tools available). That's a day of consulting fees at anything upwards of $150 to $270 per hour.

This doesn't even account for the lost productivity of those staff, which is going to be around 3x the revenue earned from your payroll! So now your actual costs are looking to be somewhere north of $25,000 for a two-day outage. You're going to be kicking yourself for not sussing your disaster recovery plan sooner.

This is why having a clear RTO matters, since it's basically a matter of how much a disaster recovery-triggering event is going to cost you.

What your RTO looks like, though, is going to vary depending on what kind of disaster recovery plan you have and what your business looks like. Businesses with dedicated servers on or off site will have to factor in the time it takes to replace hardware and restore a server, for instance.

Between hardware replacements and lost productivity, you can easily see thousands of dollars disappear because of a single incident.

RECOVERY POINT OBJECTIVE (RPO)

You'll have undoubtedly been working on an important file at some point in your life only to have the computer unexpectedly shut down and all your work disappear before your eyes. Ideally the autosave function will have been working away in the background, ensuring that a copy of your work has been filed away safely during your work; if not, hopefully you'll have been hitting that 'Save' button regularly enough so that when you gingerly turn on the computer, you're presented with a file not too far off what you've just been working on.

If your RTO is how much time you're prepared to absorb between an incident and recovery, then your Recovery Point

Objective (RPO) is how much time – and data – you're prepared to lose between the most recent back-up and an incident.

RPOs rely on archived data and record backups that your IT professionals can draw on in the event of a disaster. Most businesses will have data on a server or system which they regularly send to a backup. This could happen every few days, or daily, hourly, every 15 minutes, once a week, or anything in between. Some will have an external hard drive that they copy over important files to every couple of weeks – or when they remember to (not ideal!).

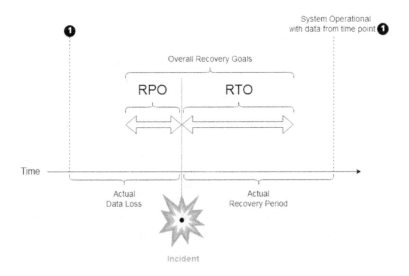

How often a business backs up their data depends on the kind of work they do and what their transaction rate looks like. An hour of transactions could be 10,000 pieces of information, or it could be 10. How much is a week worth, then?

Your recovery point is the point in time when it becomes painful for you to go back in time and recover. That's why you want as short an RPO as is reasonable for the work you do. If you're entering in the odd document then you could probably handle having daily backups rather than ones every quarter hour; if you can only afford to go back one hour before re-entering data becomes painful, then your RPO has to been less than an hour.

RETENTION

So, you're making regular backups of your data. How long do you hold onto the backups for?

This is another case when it depends on your industry and what you'd like to do with the data long-term. For some businesses, data retention in the order of days is more than suitable; others need weeks or months. Accountants and lawyers need to be able to go back seven years into their records, so for them, saving the better part of a decade's worth of files is necessary.

My go-to minimum is at least two months. 30 days is a common retention time that backup systems hold – but it's also the amount of time some malware waits in the wings before implementing. That might mean every copy is compromised. You can generally beat the malware at its own game by retaining backups for two months, and while you'll lose some data, the malware won't have gotten its tendrils into everything.

Of course, retention and disaster planning go hand in hand with team training, software and hardware updates, and a robust data security system. They're all equally important parts of your business continuity puzzle and each need time and care to ensure they're going to weather what cybercriminals, human error and hardware failure are going to throw at them.

FOLLOW THE 3-2-1 RULE

If you want any chance of surviving a cyberattack or need to protect your business's data from human error, then you need to follow the 3-2-1 Rule.

Keep 3 copies of any critical data

Only having one copy of critical data isn't going to be enough to save you from attack or system failure. As we've seen with the

30-day retention malware problem, a single backup could get ruined with a single hit. If your data is lost or corrupted, then a secondary backup is going to save your business's continuity.

Store your data in 2 different formats

You need to back up files in two different formats (at least). This helps protect against malware and ransomware that targets one particular format and encrypts all files of one particular type. This is where that secondary or tertiary backup is a help, but if a file type is damaged, inaccessible, or at risk from further attacks, you're back up that creek without that paddle.

Have 1 backup off site

The off-site backup covers you for the worst-case scenario if your one dedicated server or hard drive fails, or if your office flooded and all your computers and hard files were lost. We hope nothing ever gets to this point, but it can and does happen, so you need to be prepared.

Think about the precious family photos that you'd hate to lose or have damaged. If you want to keep them safe from accidents or attacks, then you might keep multiple copies of your photos, in physical and digital formats, with a backup on a thumb drive safely in a drawer at work, for example. That's the 3-2-1 Rule in action.

With your IT systems and critical data, the 3-2-1 Rule might involve keeping the hard copy original and a digital copy in the office, with a third copy of data held off-site.

AN IMPORTANT NOTE ABOUT CLOUD-BASED DRIVES

The 3-2-1 Rule and critical back-ups are simple enough to get in place, and many businesses already have made steps in the right direction. But equally, many businesses – especially SMEs – fall short, often by relying on cloud-based syncing drives like Google Drive, Dropbox and OneDrive.

This is something I mentioned briefly at the end of Chapter Two. Syncing drives like these might be great for working across teams, but they aren't suitable 'backups' for the kind of robust data security and handling we consider. What they do well is take the same file format and put it elsewhere – after all, it's just a hard drive in another location.

If you suffer a malware attack, then your local files are going to get encrypted – and then your cloud drive is going to sync it up. After all, they tend to autosave every few seconds. You might have thousands of files, which you can sometimes restore through the user interface, but your productivity is going to take a serious hit if you have to spend hours right-clicking and selecting 'Restore previous version' to every single file.

Don't let me scare you off cloud drives, though. For many businesses, they're becoming part of how we do work. The automatic syncing can be your data's downfall, however. If you do want to use a cloud to back up your data, then it's necessary to put some distance between the cloud and the automatic syncing service to reduce the chance of corruption or loss – not just in one location but everywhere.

DEVELOPING YOUR DISASTER RECOVERY PLAN

Whatever strategy you're developing, your disaster recovery plan has to make sense for your business, which is why it needs to be developed closely with the systems, resources and people in place to ensure the least business interruption.

As I mentioned earlier, the duration of your RTO should depend on what your time-cost balance looks like. If you start bleeding your business after two hours of downtime and your staff are waiting for computer systems to come back online, then having a disaster recovery plan that takes two days to implement is two days of business lost.

Disaster recovery is also about reviewing your backup procedures. You need to have your backups tested regularly, for instance, so that you know that they're working. I've seen companies whose backup storage devices were switched off for a year: the systems had been alerting users that it was backing up to a drive, but nothing was happening. All the while, they'd been swapping that drive back and forth with their external drive off-site. If they'd suffered an attack, they would have lost a year's records.

Reviewing and testing is equally about being sure that whoever's in charge of your backups can implement them rapidly in the RPO time that's been set. The person who oversaw backups (but hadn't tested them in a year) wasn't monitoring the process and making it happen.

Like so much of your cybersecurity, developing your disaster recovery plan isn't set and forget; it's an ongoing process. If you develop a system, and it turns out during the testing that your current model isn't going to fit for your business, then adjust it accordingly. Check out our Disaster Pplanning Checklist as a good starting point.

DO I NEED CYBERSECURITY INSURANCE?

I get asked this from time to time when clients have just signed up to our plans with our cybersecurity guarantee and my answer is this metaphor. Your business is a bus driving up a steep mountainous hill side. My team helps you keep the business on the road climbing that mountain of success by making sure the driver knows where the pot holes are, that you have a spare tyre ready to go, and there are guard rails there. But sooner or later someone will accidentally crash through the barrier despite our best efforts. You still want that ambulance at the bottom of the hill!

We recommend that owners call their insurance broker and pointedly ask them what their coverage is like with respect to cybersecurity. We have seen dramatically different business interruption policies which exclude any kind of cybersecurity claims and some which have very big loopholes which could exclude your claim.

The best value in a good cybersecurity insurance policy is in the assistance you can claim to help you with forensics, root cause analysis, remediation and most importantly dealing with the public relations campaign and communications side of informing your clientele. You'll need it to recover from the reputational damage that could seriously affect your business recovery in the wake of a serious confidentiality breach.

DISASTER PLANNING CHECKLIST

Important! This checklist should only be used as a starting point for your disaster recovery plan. This is in no way complete; we highly recommend you engage with a professional IT firm to map out a complete disaster recovery plan for your business.

Risk Assessment

□ Define all critical functions, systems, software, and data in your organisation.

□ Prioritise the above items in order of importance to your business (mission critical to minor) based on which ones, if destroyed, would have the greatest negative impact on your business.

□ Create a document that outlines your current IT infrastructure (network documentation) so another IT person or company could take over easily if your current IT person wasn't available, or could assist in the recovery of your IT infrastructure in the event of a disaster.

□ Determine the RTO (recovery time objective), RPO (recovery point objective) and MTO (maximum tolerable outage) for every critical function and system in your business.

□ Identify all threats that could potentially disrupt or destroy the above mentioned data, systems, functions, etc. and the likelihood of those threats.

Mitigation and Planning Strategies

□ Create an IT Assets Inventory list and identify all the functions, data, hardware, and systems in your business.

☐ Identify all potential disasters and threats to these systems and functions.

☐ For each mission-critical system or function, brainstorm ways to minimise, avoid, or limit the damage done.

☐ For the most likely disasters, create a disaster recovery plan specific to what damage could be done (tornado flattens your office, city evacuation, virus attack, etc.), and identify who will be responsible for executing the plan (your disaster recovery team).

☐ Identify a recovery plan and timeline for each function, and prioritise these functions by the order in which they need to be recovered if multiple mission-critical functions are affected.

☐ Create a backup strategy for your data and systems.

☐ Create a testing and validation strategy, and schedule tests for your backups.

☐ Define your communication plan in the event of a disaster to employees, clients, vendors, and the media.

☐ Create a 'break the glass' document that contains instructions on what to do if a key executive dies, is disabled, or is otherwise unavailable for a long period of time.

☐ Review your current insurance policy to make sure you have sufficient coverage to replace the assets in your organisation.

☐ Define a media communication strategy (how you will communicate with the press if a disaster happens).

☐ Summarise this into a disaster recovery plan and brief the disaster recovery team on the plan.

☐ Schedule a periodic meeting to review and update the plan with your disaster recovery team.

A CLOSER LOOK: DISASTER RECOVERY IN ACTION

Recovery is more than just protecting your business's data. It can also save your business serious money. One of our clients is a service provider who has some understandably heavy-duty hardware in place to service their customers. That hardware can be attractive for a scammer – and particularly for cryptocurrency mining.

Cryptocurrency and the way it's produced require a book of their own, but for now what's important is that the currencies are made and minted through a lot of complex, CPU-hungry calculations. And it's lucrative. On January 4, 2017, the value of a Bitcoin (by far the most popular digital currency) reached its peak, a staggering ~$1,600 NZD.

Our client came to us because their ~200 machines were running slow and hot. They could tell a staffer had used a remote access tool to install cryptomining software on their machines, sponging up their resources to make untraceable digital money like Bitcoin. Among the problems like slower servers, maxed-out CPUs running hot, increased power consumption, a higher chance of machine failure and the fact that someone was out there making money off their machines means that our client was quick to find the culprit. The company also had to deal with the fact that the culprit could have been one of several people. If no one person were to face up, then the seeds of distrust in the organisation start getting sown.

Thankfully for our client, they had comprehensive backups of their systems, and we were able to together look back at their email system and look for activations of remote access tools and software. We found evidence of activation via email to a personal device, which the staffer had then purged from the system and removed future evidence of.

The company got that one person in the room and challenged them. They resigned on the spot.

One of the lesser-known reasons for a backup is that it gives the business an incredible opportunity to look back in time and see a valid copy of what data was like, as well as what it is like now. As your workforce gets bigger, so do your risks; from a cybersecurity perspective, being sure of what's going on behind the scenes is your safety net and your guarantee.

6

CONCLUSION: MOVING FORWARD

BY NOW, YOU MIGHT BE FEELING that cybersecurity's a bit daunting, but that's not a reason to throw out all your electronics and live in a commune!

I'm deep into cybersecurity every day. I see the worst of what people do – and try to do – to each other through the weak spots in their security. The malware battering at the gates, the threats and promises, the well-meaning dollars going out the door. Even with all this going on, and a lot of effort to hold it at bay, I still think technology is brilliant. Take it from me.

It makes our lives easier by doing the hard jobs for us; it allows us to work faster, communicate instantly with the rest of the world, and create really interesting solutions to some of the big problems out there. As I said at the start of this book, the world we're living in is digital, so being safe and keeping Kiwi businesses thriving is about digital – and real-world – solutions.

I started Vertech over a decade ago because I saw too many Kiwi businesses failing to do the minimum to secure their IT and their data against digital threats. They were racing forward in other aspects, doing great work and helping our economy grow – but they were doing it without the cybersecurity to protect them, and safely thrive. So, when something hits – and it is a when, not an if – the business and its staff soon suffer.

With the passing of the Privacy Act 2020, there are now mandatory privacy breach notification requirements. That means companies can't sweep attacks under the rug and hope no one will notice. It also means that we can better understand the realities of scams, spam and extortions, and that failing to invest sufficiently to protect your and your client's data could lead to an extinction level event for your business!

CYBERSECURITY REALITY 1: YOU'VE GOT TO LAYER UP

As we've seen, developing robust cybersecurity – and keeping your cash and maintaining your work and your reputation – is really a matter of smaller elements working together. So, you can't rely on just a firewall, antivirus, or the best practices of your team. Single point solutions are just that – single obstacles to block specific vectors of attack. It's when they are combined that they shine.

Remember, the eight essential layers of cybersecurity are:

Spam filtering

The security that prevents unsolicited and unwanted messages getting in.

Firewalls

Monitors your incoming and outgoing traffic for anything suspect.

Web filtering

Controls who can access what websites and content, and when.

Antivirus & endpoint protection

Identifies and neutralises threats that make it in via emails, websites, downloads or USB devices.

Operating systems and updates

Prevent old operating systems' vulnerabilities from getting exploited.

Ongoing staff education

Getting the people who do the clicking, downloading, and visiting educated on what to do – and more importantly, what not to do.

Password management

Keeping your sensitive passwords updated and private from everyone.

Comprehensive backups

Just in case your data gets wiped. Remember: 3 copies of any critical data in 2 different formats with 1 off-site, just in case you suffer a serious breach and loss.

CYBERSECURITY REALITY 2: IT NEVER ENDS

Think of cybersecurity as an arms race between the best software developers and security experts, and their opposing numbers within the community of state-sponsored bad actors, cybercriminals and hackers. Each are constantly working out new techniques to outfox the other.

Because technology is relatively cheap, cybercriminal activity is lucrative, and people are greedy, cybercriminals will always be active, constantly challenging the latest systems and exploiting gaps in old systems. That's why you can't just 'set and forget' your cybersecurity – you have to keep it updated, relevant and secure from all potential threats.

That starts with fixing bugs and patching software, but it also extends to upgrading your hardware, operating systems and software as they age. Running old unsupported software is a bit like failing to replacing the tyres on your car as they wear out. One day it will be raining and your car won't be able to stay on the road during a tight turn.

The antivirus program you bought three years ago might be getting its daily updates, but unless you've upgraded it to the current best version you will be missing out on whole new modules of protection the security company has bolted on as new attack vectors are discovered.

And you have to keep doing it. As long as you have a computer, you need to keep on top of updates and the latest security releases, otherwise the cybercriminals will catch you.

CYBERSECURITY REALITY 3: YOU GET WHAT YOU PAY FOR

When it comes to cybersecurity, cheap isn't best. Some businesses don't want to shell out for quality hardware, software, security or backups; they go for the cheapest solutions (aka 'free' software, or nothing at all), and don't commit to reliable security (see also: the little black book of passwords). Yes you can get free antivirus software that may protect you from 80% of threats but those 80% of threats are the historical ones. It's the current 20% that you really have to worry about! That's the house of straw approach. You need brick – with reinforcements!

Some years back, I carried the mindset that my clients' primary need was value for money, or the least-cost approach. Over time I realised that this resulted in solutions that didn't go the distance. My clients, who never once asked for the cheapest, would look to us and ask us how they still suffered malware attacks.

That's when I realised that we should be offering the best protection they can afford and work back from there. The results have been a great deal less disconcerting!

The most important thing is finding the best cybersecurity system that suits your needs and budget. The best protection if you've got cloud-based servers – i.e. an emphasis on antiviral and network security – is different than if you have servers on site (i.e. which would also include physical access security measures). The goal really is to ensure that your business is not seen as the unlocked house on your street, so go for the best protection you can afford and review this regularly to see what else could be done.

It takes a thorough assessment from a cybersecurity professional to assess your individual needs, so reach out and get a comprehensive plan made up today.

CYBERSECURITY REALITY 4: YOU'RE GOING TO MAKE MISTAKES

And that's okay. One of your team is going to click on the wrong link, visit the wrong website, or plug in a USB they found on the street.

Most businesses hire smart people, but you can't assume they know everything about the software you use, or that they haven't got some bad habits or missing knowledge that's going to compromise your security.

We've seen people within our own team get scammed! Sometimes it can just be a case of the right message getting through to the right person at the right time of day.

So, just as you've got to be up to speed on cybersecurity awareness training to keep your team situationally aware, you've got to be on top of your IT security. Breach tactics are only getting more sophisticated, as are the software and the methodologies designed to keep out the bad guys.

The trick is to not make it easy for them. Put verification processes in place for key things like suppliers' bank account number changes or anywhere else where large payments may take place.

But even if you've mastered all the other aspects of cybersecurity, someone's bound to make an honest mistake at some point. That why layering up is so important – including those back-ups at the heart of a good strategy. If someone does access a dodgy site, then the firewall is going to kick in – and the antivirus software is going to help clean things up.

Better yet, though, is to not click that suspicious link. But if you do, then the last thing you want your people to do is to hide their mistake hoping no one notices. Put processes in place to let your team know that there is a NO-BLAME culture with respect to reporting security issues, dodgy emails or suspicious activity. If they fail to report a successful or near-miss scam, then their mate two desks down may fall foul of the exact same message the next day. Their harvested login may be used to spam all of your clients. Or, in the nightmare scenario, they unwittingly grant a cybercriminal a backdoor which results in a complex ransomware attack that compromises your backups and infiltrates all your confidential data.

CYBERSECURITY REALITY 5: YOU'VE GOT TO BACK UP YOUR DATA

I get it – it's handy to have all your data in one place, right there on the desktop! And believe me, I know how much easier life would be without having to constantly be on top of backups. But you're toast if something happens to that hardware. If it only takes one lost laptop, ransomware attack or flooded server to sink your IT capability, then that's going to be a big problem.

Remember the 3-2-1 rule, which is like any strategy against interruption or disaster. The contingency plan. The 'What if' for data or server loss. Make this your mantra:

Keep **3** copies of any critical data

Use **2** different formats for data storage

Have **1** backup off site

And most important of all: frequently test that your backups actually work! This will tell you if you can recover, how quickly you can recover, and what the disruption impact will be. As you grow your business, this aspect should also be reassessed; what is acceptable when you are a team of five is incredibly painful for a business of 30 with tight time frames to deliver on contracts.

I had a prospect who dutifully changed the offsite backup drive on their local backup appliance, daily swapping it out and driving it home each day. They thought that they were 100% sorted. They became our client when I pointed out that their offsite backup contained NOTHING – the backup appliance had been simply switched off for over 12 months and their IT company never alerted them!

CYBERSECURITY REALITY 6: YOUR DATA IS YOUR REPUTATION

Data breaches happen every day, and most of them go unreported. When they do make the news, it's because it's happened to massive companies like Target, Facebook or a government. Their reputations suffer from it – though being huge enterprises, they can weather to a certain extent some bigger hits.

But what happens when a small business with tight margins loses its customers' credit card details, addresses or buying histories? What happens when their install calendars get wiped and they don't know whose houses they're supposed to be visiting?

The attacks on and breaches of smaller companies' data – like the SMEs that are the backbone of the NZ economy – often don't get noticed for 191 days (on average!), but also tend to go under-reported, not least of all because a breach can seriously damage the public's trust in how a business operates. Customers will no longer trust you. Your own employees likely won't trust you either, especially if their personal data is on the line, not to mention their reputation. Keeping your data secure is absolutely vital to protecting your business – and your people.

For our business, I tell new hires that our clients may forgive us for small mistakes like being late or misspelling their name on a ticket, but a customer will never forgive us for losing their data. Even if we don't lose them as a client, then they will never trust us fully again – and deservedly so.

CYBERSECURITY REALITY 7: YOU ARE GOING TO NEED HELP

The more we rely on digital tech for our daily operations, the more we need to be sure about how we're keeping it secure. And while we want to think breaches happen only to big players, the reality is that SMEs and private users are also getting conned, abused and cheated out of billions every year. We just hear about it less because there are no media dollars in it!

As we've seen with the Privacy Act 2020 additions, the penalties for getting hit and hiding a privacy breach can hurt you even more. Industries either self-regulate or they will increasingly come under government scrutiny. Industrial sectors such as government, healthcare, and finance are pushing complicated sounding security frameworks such as ISO 27001, NIST, HISO, HIPAA, SOC2, ASD8 etc. We haven't covered those in this book but they will come to be the standards by which you must comply in order to play the game with your upstream partners, suppliers, and clients. It's worth working with people you trust who will stay in the know on all the complex regulations!

It doesn't help that it's too easy to stick our heads in the sand and pretend it's not a problem – especially if it hasn't happened to you yet, or if the complexity is too overwhelming. But no matter where you are and what you're doing with your IT, someone out there is looking for weaknesses in your systems and trying to get in the door. The answer is actually very simple: just get me on the blower or arrange to go for a coffee.

It's our job to put up a fight. Because we are the only Managed Services IT Provider in Auckland to offer a 100% Money Back Cyber Security Guarantee, we truly do take on the risks on your behalf when you engage with us.

Our mission has always been to support entrepreneurs to grow their businesses and enable them to flexibly scale without getting IT speed wobbles. We look after systems so that you can pursue profit.

By this point, I hope you can see why I'm so passionate about cybersecurity – and why it's so important to get it right. Since I started Vertech, it's been our goal to make sure our clients have the tools to stay protected against the number one threat businesses face whilst providing the systems & infrastructure to have them be competitive in today's digital world.

After all, if you're a SME owner who's worked hard and built a profitable business that supports your staff, then you don't want to have that threatened because of lax practices, dumb mistakes, or sloppy security. A single incident can lead to a multiyear delay in you achieving your business dreams and goals.

Whether you come to us at Vertech – and I hope you do – or go to another IT security provider, make sure that they can handle all the aspects we've talked about in this book and keep an eye on the big picture. It's all well and good to have a company provide you with a flashy antivirus, but if they can't make that work well with staff education, filtering and all the others, then they're only doing part of the job.

That's why I wrote this book – so that you'd know the right questions and the right measures to ask you need in place to keep your data safe and your business running. With that in mind, I also hope you've gained some insights on cybersecurity, and had a chance to reflect on your own security situation and see where it needs improvement. And if you already have an IT provider, I hope you have a better idea of whether or not they're doing a good job!

For a clear picture of where you still have gaps – and what you can do about those gaps – visit www.vertech.co.nz/book to access a 30 minute cybersecurity assessment with the Vertech team (free for you as a reader of this book!).

Every business deserves to be secure and have their own and their customers' data protected. Luckily, cybersecurity doesn't have to be hard – not if you and your IT experts know what to do. It's time to form your defences, train your team, and set off on your path towards having a super-secure business.

Good luck!

ABOUT THE AUTHOR

DANIEL WATSON has been helping businesses keep secure and running smoothly as the owner/operator of Vertech IT Services since 2010. His specialties include cybersecurity, creative IT solutions, business development, and out-of-the-box technical solutions.

He has been sharing his cybersecurity and IT advice with Kiwi businesses via LinkedIn and Youtube for several years, and is now excited to provide small business owners with an actionable guide to protecting their businesses through his first book, *She'll Be Right (Not!)*.

Married with two teenage children, Daniel is actively involved as a Watch Assistant volunteer with the Spirit of Adventure Trust, as a leader in the local Sea Scouts Troop, and was a Sergeant with the Royal New Zealand Engineering Corps Army Reserve.

FOLLOW Daniel Watson through Linkedin
https://www.linkedin.com/in/daniel-watson-smb-cybersecurity-expert-07424b12

LEARN MORE about Vertech - www.vertech.co.nz

in

RESOURCES

CERT NZ, Quarter Two Report 2019
   https://www.cert.govt.nz/about/quarterly-report/quarter-two-report-2019/ww

CERT NZ, 2018 Report Summary
   https://www.cert.govt.nz/about/quarterly-report/summary-report-2018/

ZD Net, Ransomware: The Key Lesson Maersk Learned from Battling the NotPetya Attack
   https://www.zdnet.com/article/ransomware-the-key-lesson-maersk-learned-from-battling-the-notpetya-attack/

WIRED, The Untold Story of NotPetya, the Most Devastating Cyberattack in History
   https://www.wired.com/story/notpetya-cyberattack-ukraine-russia-code-crashed-the-world/

Verizon Enterprise Solutions, 2019 DBIR Summary of Findings
   https://enterprise.verizon.com/resources/reports/dbir/2019/summary-of-findings/>

Forbes, Cybercriminals Have Your Business In Their Crosshairs And Your Employees Are In Cahoots With Them
https://www.forbes.com/sites/ivywalker/2019/01/31/cybercriminals-have-your-business-their-crosshairs-and-your-employees-are-in-cahoots-with-them/#28fb4f751953

Ministry of Business, Innovation and Employment (MBIE) NZ, Small Business
https://www.mbie.govt.nz/business-and-employment/business/support-for-business/small-business/

National Initiative for Cybersecurity Careers and Studies, National Cybersecurity Awareness Month 2019
https://niccs.us-cert.gov/about-niccs/national-cybersecurity-awareness-month-2019

The Guardian, Huge Rise in Hacking Attacks on Home Workers during Lockdown
https://www.theguardian.com/technology/2020/may/24/hacking-attacks-on-home-workers-see-huge-rise-during-lockdown

Check Point Software, COVID-19 Impact: Cyber Criminals Target Zoom Domains
https://blog.checkpoint.com/2020/03/30/covid-19-impact-cyber-criminals-target-zoom-domains/

The Hacker News, Hackers Created Thousands of Coronavirus (COVID-19) Related Sites As Bait
https://thehackernews.com/2020/03/covid-19-coronavirus-hacker-malware.html

GET YOUR FREE 'LUNCH + LEARN' AND FREE 30-MIN CYBERSECURITY CONSULTATION TODAY

IF YOU WANT TO KEEP SAFE, then you've got to stay ahead of cybercriminals. Because you've read this book, you can also get access to one of our 'Lunch + Learn' sessions, plus you'll receive a free 30-minute cybersecurity consultation to discover where your business might be vulnerable, and the areas you could improve to make your business more secure.

Visit vertech.co.nz/book to access it today.